Conditioning4Excellence
Your Success is in YOU . . . LET'S GET IT!

Principles for cultivating your best:

MIND, BODY, & SPIRIT

Conditioning4Excellence
Your Success is in YOU . . . LET'S GET IT!

By Tim Watson

Coaching you to successful:
- **Friendships**
- **Families**
- **Careers**
- **Love**
- **Fitness**
- **Finances**

authorHOUSE®

AuthorHouse™
1663 Liberty Drive
Bloomington, IN 47403
www.authorhouse.com
Phone: 1-800-839-8640

First published by AuthorHouse   08/05/2011

ISBN: 978-1-4634-3513-4 (sc)
ISBN: 978-1-4634-3515-8 (hc)
ISBN: 978-1-4634-3514-1 (ebk)

Library of Congress Control Number: 2011912483

Printed in the United States of America

This book is printed on acid-free paper.

Because of the dynamic nature of the Internet, any web addresses or links contained in this book may have changed since publication and may no longer be valid. The views expressed in this work are solely those of the author and do not necessarily reflect the views of the publisher, and the publisher hereby disclaims any responsibility for them.

This publication is designed to provide general information regarding the subject matter covered. However, laws, guidelines, and practices often vary from state to state and are subject to change. Because each factual situation is different, specific advice should be tailored to the particular circumstances. For this reason, the reader is advised to consult with his or her own advisor regarding their specific situation.

Scripture quotations are from the New International Version Study Bible, 10th Anniversary Edition. Copyright 1995 by Zondervan Publishing House; and the New American Standard Ryrie Study Bible Expanded Edition. Copyright 1986, 1995 by The Moody Bible Institute of Chicago.

The author and publisher have taken reasonable precautions in the preparation of this book and believe the facts presented in the book are accurate as of the date it was written. However, neither the author nor the publisher assumes any responsibility for any errors or omissions. The author and publisher specifically disclaim any liability resulting from the use or application of the information contained in this book, and the information is not intended to serve as legal, financial, or other professional advice related to individual situations.

For information about special discounts for bulk purchases, or to schedule an engagement for Tim Watson to visit your organization, contact Sales & Booking Coordinator of UPLIFT Systems, LLC at info@upliftsystems.com.

CONTENTS

SECTION V
SYSTEMS OF EXCELLENCE

CKNOWLEDGEMENTS

There are so many influential people who have made a huge impact on my life that it would possibly fill the entire content of a book to list them all. However, there are certainly those of whom I'm consciously aware who I know God intentionally placed in my path in order that I might receive the wisdom He imparted through them. First and foremost, I would like to acknowledge and thank my parents James Timothy Watson, Sr. and Mattie Bell Watson for the uncompromising leadership they have provided my entire life. Next, I would like to thank my teachers (both formal and informal) who were principled enough to not let me settle for good, and challenged me to be great: Ms. Taylor, Mrs. Hawkins, Mrs. Dixon, Mrs. Robinson, Mrs. Miller, Mrs. Vinson, and Mrs. Washington, thanks for your steadfast guidance. To the coaches who mentored beyond the playing field: the late Eugene Abrams, the late Lee Forehand, Eddie Mullins, William Moultrie, Roger Jackson, Rubin Carter, Steve Wilson, Ron Springs, Herm Edwards, and Emmitt Thomas, thank you for helping nurture in my manhood, and encouraging my tenacity. I would like to thank my children for inspiring elements of manhood unattained through any other medium besides fatherhood: Tré James Timothy Watson, Alexus Jasmine Watson, and Christian Justus Watson, it was the arrival of you three that introduced me to the true meaning of love. Last, but certainly not least, I would like to thank my wife Audrey, who has challenged me to be the best man I can be. Through my fallible manhood I realize God even guided me through my prior relationship decisions, and BLESSED THE BROKEN ROAD THAT LED ME STRAIGHT TO YOU. It's you who inspired the completion of this work that has been in the makings my entire life.

N IDEA IS BORN

In October of 2007 after experiencing a sudden onset of excruciating abdominal pain my father was found to have a mysteriously twisted colon. During emergency surgery a portion was cut out and he was temporarily fitted with a colostomy bag. Not even a week into his recovery, my mother's doctor told her that she had breast cancer. This was the second untimely attack by this deadly disease on my parents. Just eight years earlier, my dad persevered bravely through months of treatments and was blessed to defeat prostate cancer. He was only fifty-four years old at the time, and the picture of great health and fitness otherwise.

As you might expect, our entire family was quite distressed. My siblings and I were befuddled trying to figure out what we could do to help our parents. Fortunately for us, the world—renowned Moffitt Cancer Center was located near my home in Tampa, Florida. We were able to get a second opinion there for my mother. Sadly, the diagnosis was confirmed. But because it is an advanced research facility, the doctors at Moffitt were able to prescribe and administer a treatment plan that gave us all confidence in her recovery.

My younger sister, Tasha (who lives in Georgia near our parents), and I shared the duties of transporting them to Moffitt every three weeks from Georgia. She would drive them from their home to the Georgia/Florida border. I would then drive the Florida leg of the journey. For over three hours each way, I was afforded many life-lessons while traversing Interstate-75 with my parents. This provided me with once-in-a-lifetime growth over those several months.

Those hours spent tapping into my parents' wisdom and experience became a truly pivotal segment of my life. By being with them, I was able to observe reciprocal love in a manner I had yet to understand. Our "windshield time" conversations greatly enhanced my appreciation of this earthly time with which I've been blessed.

Every moment of this challenge was a moment that my parents faced and conquered together. During countless doctor's visits, chemotherapy sessions, and radiation treatments, my Dad never left her side. The first eight weeks of treatment, my father accompanied her with a disconnected colon and a colostomy bag in tow. Likewise, my mom was present at each of my dad's appointments, and his colon reattachment surgery as well. Immediately following each of the chemotherapy treatments in Tampa, they would tell me about the inspiring conversations they had with other patients. I met many of these people also at Moffitt, and they would share what a great attitude my mom had, and how their spirits were lifted by the conversations my parents had with them. My mother was definitely an inspiration to others. She often stated without hesitation to people saddened by her illness, *"Don't worry about me . . . I'm not sick, I've just been diagnosed with cancer . . . and I'm in the hands of One who's bigger than cancer, for I'm blessed and highly favored!"* Now that is *Excellent Attitude 101.*

Additionally, they imparted to me practical wisdom that changed my life. For many years I didn't understand how my parents seemed so *happy* all the time. They often lived check to check, and haven't experienced the *American Dream* of financial freedom. I have myself enjoyed many of the finer—material—things in life, and oftentimes travel in circles of other people who live financially well. To a degree, I in my young adulthood had equated material wealth to success. I have of course been able to share some of my resources with my parents. However, when I was ready and able to grasp the concept, they explained to me what fueled their persistent joy, and the real meaning of living successfully. Though they are proud of who I am, they want me to know that the material things are not what they view as true success. Success to them is actualizing one's purpose. My father shared that he and my mom believe they are called to be "people's people." He explained that even within their meager means, their purpose here on earth has been to "cater to anyone in need of help in whatever way they've been able to provide help over the years." Living this calling the best they know how keeps them happy, and gives them an incomparable feeling of success. They truly believe that the most valuable things we as human beings can give or receive, cannot be purchased with dollars and cents. Listening to this as their son, I felt I was experiencing the epitome of the biblical verse Romans 8:28, *"And we know that in all things God works for the good of those who love Him, who have been called according to His purpose."*

In what appeared to be the direst of circumstances, we became closer than ever. The outpouring of love and support from those in the community whose lives my parents had touched over the years was overwhelming. The degree of selflessness with which these two people have lived their lives was on full display. People from near and far began reconnecting with our family to express their heartfelt concern.

That these two people persevered through this colossal challenge with smiles on their faces comes as no surprise to anyone close to "The Dynamic Two". The fact is, they have been nothing short of amazing to all they've touched. I am routinely contacted by old grade-school buddies who share stories about how they were impacted positively by something my parents had done. To this very day, many call and check in, or stop by to say hello, when they're in town.

It became clear why my parents live with such resolve and excellent attitudes, despite circumstances that might have tried their conviction. They have unwavering faith and trust in a relationship they had established long ago with their Lord and Savior Jesus Christ. They in turn share the fruit of that relationship with all whom they come into contact. My parents certainly have been called according to God's purpose. Thankfully, I'm a first-hand recipient of the fruit of their calling. With a new appreciation for the value of my time here on earth, I was also able to make some decisions that have been critical in actualizing my life's purpose as well.

I'm happy to report that after intensive chemotherapy, surgery, and radiation treatments, on March 26, 2008 my mother's pathology test results showed she was, and remains cancer free. Additionally, my father has recovered completely and is 100% back to his normal activities. Normal for him is, at 65, going on a 10-mile jog to celebrate his birthday, followed by putting young people in the gym to shame. All who work out with him have to be ready to bring excellence. I still recall the wonderful times he and I shared as he served as my training partner preparing for college football (in 1988), and later for my first NFL training camp (in 1993).

While we were training together, we would rise four days a week at 3:00AM for our workouts. This schedule was maintained for ten weeks at a time. Although I had already nurtured a serious work ethic, there was still nothing like the motivation of having my father running stride for stride and lifting rep after rep with me. We invited other relatives, friends, and old teammates of mine along for the experience as well. None of them had ever experienced that level of training difficulty.

The experience provided a lesson in attrition and clear evidence why of the approximately 1.2 million high school football players, only 54,000 make it to college; and only 1800 men grace the NFL fields annually. Of the five invitees to our training sessions, only one survived either of the two periods. The lone survivor, my cousin Chris, was able to go have a highly productive College football career on a full scholarship. As for my dad, who was forty-two and forty-seven years old respectively when we were training, he never missed a single stride or rep.

As I began researching and gathering information for this book, I was reminded of the foundation laid for me by the most loving, selfless, trusting, respectful, and unbreakable relationship that I know: the marriage of my parents, James Timothy Watson, Sr. and Mattie Bell Watson. They aren't perfect people. They have made their fair share of mistakes in life. However, they have demonstrated the epitome of executing with excellence—particularly so in establishing fruitful and lasting relationships, one of the most crucial ingredients to a purposeful life. With all my heart, I thank you both for nurturing me into the man I am today, and the man I'll become tomorrow. I know that the "work" is always in progress. Most of all though, I want to thank you for introducing me to the most important relationship in my life: my Lord and Savior Jesus Christ!

My Parents: Mattie Bell Watson & James T. Watson, Sr.

SECTION I:

FOUNDATION

Chapter 1

he UPLIFT Objective

The primary objective of this book is to provide all who read it with UPLIFT personally and professionally. It shares principles designed to be systematically followed in order to live a successful life. Strategically organized to form **Systems of Excellence™ (SOE),** these principles will help raise your mind, body, and spirit to higher levels.

Systems are organized sets of interrelated principles, ideas, and/or processes used to achieve specific objectives. Excellence is 100% effort while executing within our areas of control. Executing with excellence is the only way to maximize the full potential of our natural talents and developed skills.

"Executing with excellence is the only way to maximize the full potential of our natural talents and developed skills."

Each of us must make a personal decision to best utilize our blessings of time, talent, and treasure. Our stewardship of these three elements is paramount to our success. They must be identified and prioritized by the individual or group in order to execute with excellence.

UPLIFT is significant beyond its literal meaning. **U**nited **P**eople **L**iving **I**n **F**oundational **T**ruth also represents components of a successful life:

- **United**—Peace is a catalyst for progress. Conflict leads to regression. Winners dwell in peace. They can be found on teams united in their objectives and in the processes necessary to achieve them. Our ability to thrive hinges on our willingness to accept and execute whatever role we may have as a member of a united team.
- **People**—Simply put, the more inclusive we are of other people in our individual life journeys, the more likely we are to be successful. This includes an ability to cultivate relationships with people of various faiths, ethnicities, cultures, and creeds.
- **Living**—This simple verb encompasses all aspects of our time on earth, whether at our vocation, play or rest. Our lives are not to be lived solely within the "box" of our natural comfort zones. If we don't risk something, we won't accomplish anything.
- **In Foundational**—It's essential that our life objectives and principles are built on a credible foundation. That which is nurtured in us will be the building blocks for what is produced by us. Our character is not a by-product of tests. It is created in our nurturing, and manifests itself during trials.
- **Truth**—Being true to oneself will be evident in our ability to live fruitfully. We will always find excellence most attainable within our own unique beliefs, inspirations, talents, and objectives.

Chapter 2

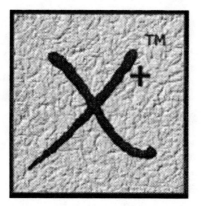

$\mathcal{T}$he X⁺ Principle™

Here, the letter X is similar to the "unknown" in algebra. No one is born knowing the impact s/he'll make on the world. We all have the free will to "solve" the X in the equation of our lives. It is our choice whether or not we remain a non-factor (an unknown "X") or make our mark on society.

"Activities done by men of evil intent will not ultimately produce positive results."

Unfortunately some have chosen to leave a negative mark. There are many "X minuses" littering the streets and filling our prisons. We even find them in presumably productive settings. X minuses are known by the negativity they leave in their wake. There's a great biblical reference that speaks to the true heart of men as is evidenced in their actions:

"For each tree is known by its own fruit. For men do not gather figs from thorns, nor do they pick grapes from a briar bush. The good man out of the good treasure of his heart brings forth what is good; and the evil man out of the evil treasure brings forth what is evil; for his mouth speaks from that which fills his heart." (Luke 6: 44-45) Activities done by men of evil intent will not ultimately produce positive results. Instead of contributing to society, these people are taking from it. By contrast, the choice of excellence is to become an X⁺ ("X plus") by making a positive impact.

It is possible for each of us to have a life of prosperity in our own way. This objective is attained by accepting nothing less than excellence. Legendary Green Bay Packers coach Vince Lombardi once shared, "The quality of a man's life is in direct proportion to his commitment to excellence, regardless of his chosen field of endeavor." Excellence is not to be confused with perfection. If perfection were our measuring stick, we would have very little chance for success.

I have been blessed to live an X+ life by design. The principles that were nurtured within me are shared within the chapters to follow. The commitment to excellence has been a team effort. It exemplifies the UPLIFT with which my life has been filled. There's a great line from the John Donne poem "Meditations XVII": "No man is an island unto himself." This speaks to how interconnected the lives of human beings are without regard to gender, ethnicity, or socio-economic class. I believe nothing great is accomplished in solitude. Excellent people together on excellent teams, executing excellent processes, will produce excellent results!

"The quality of a man's life is in direct proportion to his commitment to excellence, regardless of his chosen field of endeavor."
-Vince Lombardi

During my travels as a speaker very few, if any, of the audience know anything about me before I am introduced. This is actually an important component of my relating to them. I've enjoyed some real-life successes, yet there is nothing especially unique about them relative to my opportunities.

In other words, I'm just a small-town kid from Fort Valley, Georgia who is blessed to have experienced many valuable and transferable life lessons.

My personal history does not consist of a tale overcoming horrible circumstances. There's certainly value in the stories of individuals who rose above at-risk childhoods to become successful. These individuals may provide the best successful personal experience with relative perspective (SPERP) to a particular audience. This book, however, promotes the results of strategic nurturing and relational involvement as I believe it should be carried out. My resources are readily available to my audiences, or to you who read this book.

Along with my successes, I've also met with presumed failure many times along my journey. In those experiences blossomed the maturity and wisdom necessary to make the correct critical choices at forks in the road. Beyond my formal training, the principles I share came from experience, dictums of my faith in Jesus Christ, and first-hand observation of mentors throughout my life.

My upbringing was modest. I'm the second of four children by a mother who provided day care in our home, and an ex-military father who chose fitness and athletics at Warner Robins AFB for his civilian career. We were a typical lower-middle-class Southern household. We didn't live extravagantly, but our needs were always met.

My parents instilled putting God first as far back as I can remember. Everything instilled by my parents was done through example. They lived their creed. When it was time to work around the house, we all worked. Conversely, when it was time to play, many times we would do things the entire family enjoyed. Additionally, my parents' interaction with others in the community was exemplary. In sum, the examples they set complemented the directives they gave.

Chapter 3

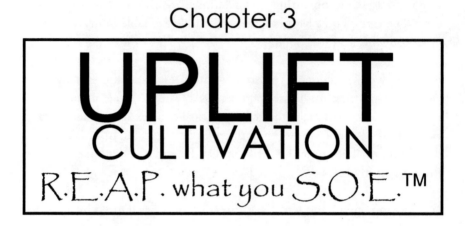

𝒯he Principle of Nurturing™

Within a God-fearing environment I was nurtured with the importance of an excellent attitude, excellent integrity, excellent work ethic, and excellent discipline. I was still, at times, as boisterous and amorous as any other inquisitive youth and young adult. For those familiar with the effectiveness of "the rod", it was NOT spared in our home. Thus, we were certainly NOT spoiled. There were certainly occasions when my immature decisions, and resulting actions, were contrary to what I was being taught at home. Thankfully though, the **Principle of Nurturing™** found within God's word continually perseveres through my intrinsically rebellious nature: *"Train a child in the way he should go, and when he is old he will not depart from it."* (Proverbs 22:6) The key word to this verse is train. In other words, in order to instill anything within anyone a consistent process must be followed.

Growing up in an area abounding with the business of agriculture provided my and other parents in Fort Valley with a great training tool for introducing work ethic. Many of us spent summers in the peach fields, and late falls harvesting pecans. Picking peaches, and carrying around full 30-40 lb. buckets in the hot sun instilled quite the perspective for what hard work really entails. We also gained a great appreciation for the value of the dollar. A day's pay in the fields was accumulated by the bucket (of peaches), or pound (of pecans). The most humbling visual that sticks in my mind to this day is the tossing of a single quarter into my bucket following each trip to have it emptied into the transport crate. These were tough days, but well worth the experiences.

Purposefully injecting challenging experiences into our lives has produced some great success stories from the approximately 8,000 residents of tiny Fort Valley, GA. Included are many successful teachers, ministers, doctors, lawyers, judges, professional athletes, engineers, and various other notable professionals. Particularly unique is the fact that we have had eight (8) players in the National Football League. That's arguably more, per capita, than any other place in America. The resulting products of this nurturing are then not by chance, but by design. Just as extraordinary diamonds are formed under pressure and over time, so are extraordinary people. It's an essential element of perseverance needed to fulfill one's ultimate individual purpose.

Of course additional *opportunities* existed for the Watson kids. Our childhood home was built on four acres of land, of which two were cleared of trees. I recall many warm-weather Saturday mornings when my brother and I were tasked with cutting the grass on the two open acres while my father chopped wood. In the falls we would have to rake leaves and pine straw from the same two acres. There seemed to always be something to do. We joke about this today, but back then we really thought my father was allergic to rest.

From this nurtured work ethic sprouted an entrepreneurial spirit. There were a number of families in my neighborhood without boys in the household. I was able to quickly gain clients among them, cutting their lawns for anywhere from $10—$20 each. My most consistent was Dr. Norma Givens, a professor from Fort Valley State College (now Fort

Valley State University). She kept me booked most weekends during the Springs and Summers until I left for college.

College provided the final seasoning during my transition from teenager to young adult. I continued my entrepreneurial efforts with a hair cutting business birthed through a freshman year Marketing Class project. I was able to make extra money cutting hair for my entire four (4) years, and my client list grew to include both males and females. By this time I had gotten a better grasp of the practical uses of the educational development that had taken place over the many years of formalized schooling. I was able to put together my own comprehensive successful business plans, write eloquent inspirational speeches, and develop experiential sales training programs. These have all been products of applying the correctly nurtured life skills with an effectively developed intellect. The barber skills served me well enough that I'm still my own most trusted barber today, as well as that of my family.

As I've watched people come and go along this journey, it's become even more evident how valuable the instilled characteristics have been for me. An ingrained positive attitude has gotten me through many challenging moments, even when I initially didn't feel so positive. The moral fiber with which my parents raised me kept me on the right track in the midst of many tempting options to venture down the wrong one. There have been a number of seemingly unbearable workloads that a groomed work ethic has allowed me to handle routinely. And my discipline to carry out my objectives to fruition has been self-evident.

As a child I remember thinking that there was no way all the hard work we were exposed to would be useful later in life. I figured it to be some form of punishment at the time. Today, I can absolutely see the privilege. High level competences for success are cultivated, not found. I thank God my parents knew better than I on ways to trigger them.

Chapter 4

The Principle of Personal Relativity™

My parents exposed me to many different interests and people at home, school, church, and in extra-curricular activities. These experiences allowed me to build meaningful relationships, evaluate my skills, and discover my passions. Then, I had to appropriately cultivate and direct each toward suitable objectives. God blessed me physically with a relatively high level of athletic talent, intellectually with gifts in the areas of analytical and literary ingenuity, and emotionally he gave me a high level of resolve. I had to direct these gifts within my passions, and toward suitable objectives.

I began my athletic development playing youth sports at the age of five. In school I was a high-achieving student. Initially though, my relational connections got in my way. Most of my buddies with whom I shared

9

extracurricular interests didn't have report cards that looked like mine. And none of us were all that big on conforming conduct. So the infamous note "talks too much" regularly appeared on my school progress reports. I was content being inappropriately placed in what was known as the Regular or Average curriculum because I wanted to hang out with my friends.

However, in 3rd Grade, one of my teachers, Mrs. Hawkins, sat me down and told me I was better than average and tested me into advanced classes. I didn't just leave my buddies behind. Mrs. Hawkins saw in me something special and pushed me to excel. I have maintained lasting friendships with some of those old school buddies to this day. I also developed new relationships with other kids with similar academics. Many of these friendships endure as well. My newer friends challenged and inspired me through a relative connection of high achievement. This was my first taste of the fruits of my **Principle of Personal Relativity**™. Simply put, we are most likely to be influenced by those individuals who have successful personal experience with a relative perspective to our own (a SPERP). We have a choice to align ourselves with individuals who have achieved success.

New discoveries and wise council have occurred often throughout my life. When it was time for me to make a college selection, I sought the advice of a number of individuals who had successfully travelled the journey upon which I was about to embark. I ended up not making the typical choice of the prize football recruit I had become. After weighing all the information I had, I chose to accept a full scholarship from Howard University over the more prominent football programs recruiting me. I was physically ready and academically gifted to thrive in any college environment. I was well versed in academic subjects and America's history. However, my small, sheltered, Southern-town upbringing didn't necessarily expose me to diverse people, different cultures, and a true knowledge of MY-story.

Interestingly, even though I grew up in relatively modern times compared to my parents' generation, we still experienced some of the lingering scars of a society not far removed from segregation and institutionalized racism. The ethnic populations of tiny Fort Valley during my youth were predominantly divided, literally, by the railroad tracks that ran down the center of the town. Church services were the factual display of the infamous observation made by both Billy Graham and Martin Luther King, Jr. that "Sunday mornings at 11AM are the most segregated hour of America's week." This was an unfortunate reality of my childhood that still exists today.

I did interact with kids of other ethnicities, but only during school, and in sports. Even so, during my high school years, sadly we had no school sponsored prom in which everyone could participate. So the White students held their own prom, and we organized our event separately. Even though we weren't coming together on our own, our administrators weren't exactly without blame in promoting the separation. The student population was actually provided ballots to vote for our Senior Superlatives and Prom Queens by ethnicity. I knew there had to be advancements in our modern society beyond such ignorance. It took venturing beyond Fort Valley to truly see the breadth of opportunities available to all people, and the inter-ethnic camaraderie that was present outside my limited exposures.

The overall dynamics of the Howard University environment brought my development to the level I needed to be a success in life—not just on the football field, or in corporate America. During my college years I was a Dean's List student, qualified for membership in the Golden Key International Honour Society, and twice was named respectively All Conference, All American, and Player of the Year. I left with seven (7) blocked kicks, which is a school record that remains today. Additionally, I was the first athlete in the history of the school to be named a GTE Academic All-American, and I was tied for the highest NFL draft pick in the history of the university. On top of all of that, I graduated with cum laude honors in four years with a dual degree in Business Marketing and Fashion Merchandising and went on to complete graduate work in Athletic Administration. As extraordinary as they are, these noteworthy accomplishments alone are still not the foundational elements for success.

Golden Key International Honour Society

Most pertinent for me were the useable life-skills I gained and the development of what I call life **REALS**. Not only did I develop intellectually. I **R**elated to diverse cultures; **E**xperientially I was exposed to more people, places, and things in four years than in my prior seventeen combined; my **A**spirations grew tremendously; **L**inguistically I became able to more accurately present my true self; and **S**piritually I gained maturity in my faith. REALS are the practical life skills that allow us to go beyond the classrooms and into the real world. It's hard for anyone to be the best s/he can possibly be without cultivating each, but it takes more than an individual effort; we need other people to actively participate in our lives. These connections will come by various means. The key is to make sure to intentionally have them. Relationships have been my foundation every step of the journey.

Howard University Hall of Fame

I've been fortunate to enjoy a few history-making successes, while persevering through, and learning from, some huge disappointments. Having traveled the path of athletics with relatively few setbacks, the ones I had were life altering. The first of these occurred during middle-school football. After becoming a bit of a Peach County Recreation Department standout on the football fields of Fort Valley and neighboring Byron, I was excited to finally get to play ball with the big boys at school. My first opportunity was my 7th grade year on our Fort Valley Middle School football team. This was Showtime! My chance had arrived to prove my wares as a legitimate player. Unlike the recreation leagues, we could not just pay to play. Each player had to try out and make the team. I was impressive enough to earn my spot, and served as a back-up at running back and linebacker to a couple of 8th graders. Although humbling in some regards, my 7th grade season went by without much of a hitch. The humbling part was the fact that I was not a starting player for the first time since I began playing organized sports. I wasn't willing to settle for being second string. However, I knew I had work to do to win the starting job and 8th Grade would be my time to shine.

The first big disappointment came before that 8th grade season ever began. Following my normal summer of laboring in the peach fields, yard work, and participation in the National Youth Sports Program at Fort Valley State College, I was excited to begin the football season. However, there would be an unexpected derailing of my plans.

Just over a month prior to the start of football try-outs my family and I took our venture to my mother's hometown of Mount Vernon, GA. We participated in the homecoming festivities held annually on the weekend leading into the first Monday in August. We were having a great time with family and friends throughout the weekend. Our final day there though would inject a challenge that changed my life. Always ready and willing to take advantage of opportunities, my regular job at the festival was at my Great Aunt Anna's concession stand during baseball games. At the close of the games we started packing and loading the concession items as usual. I received my day's pay from Aunt Anna while we closed shop. Excited about a lucrative day of work, the other kids and I were having fun and playing as dusk drew near on another great "First Monday in August."

A friendly challenge followed by an amazing feat of athleticism would turn my elation into agony. I had many times throughout my youth demonstrated interesting physical talents. This night provided one of those forums. The other kids didn't think I could jump from the ground over the tailgate and onto the back of a pick-up truck. After being dared to show what I could do, I gladly took the challenge. With a short run and jump, the feat was accomplished with relative ease. However, the landing was not in the plans. My left foot ended up splashing into a pot of scalding-hot boiled peanuts that had been placed just on the other side of the tailgate. The pain was excruciating, but I didn't realize the degree to which I was injured until I snatched off my shoe and sock, and saw the skin surrounding my ankle dripping as if it was a liquid. My family rushed me to the emergency room and I was found to have suffered a third-degree burn. Of course this would require extensive therapy and healing time.

As horrible as was the initial pain of the burn, the therapy sessions were worse. A couple of times a week my parents had to take me in for treatments. The therapists would scrub the wound with something that resembled a scouring pad soaked in betadine solution. I was told that it was necessary to prevent infection and promote healing. For me at just short of 13 years old, it was almost unbearable. But I knew I had to do it in order to be ready for football season.

My mother did the best she could, with her usual tenderness and empathy, to prepare me for the possibility I may not be able to play that year. Ever persistent, I was unwilling to give up on my 8th grade football season. So when training camp rolled around, I was right in the middle of the action. The week-long try-outs were a part of the process in which I felt I needed to participate. Although hobbled by the ankle injury I didn't miss a single session. When the pre-season practices ended it was time to reveal the players who made the team. We all waited in anticipation of the school's office announcing the final roster, prior to Coach Barfield posting it in the main hall way.

As the names were read in alphabetical order, my excitement was elevated with each passing one. With the beginning letter of my last name, I was accustomed to such anticipation during alphabetical announcements, often being one of the last people called. However, this time didn't have the expected ending. My name was never called. All of my friends and classmates stared in my direction for a response. I was stunned. Some of them were in more disbelief than even I. Still, unwilling to accept that my name was not on the list, my friends and I awaited the posting in the hall way. At that point the confirmation was made. I did not make the team. My heart was broken, and I could hardly function the rest of the day. I had my mother come pick me up from school early because I couldn't bear having the other students see the sobbing I knew I wasn't going to be able to hold back for very long. As soon as my mother arrived I broke down in her arms crying like I hadn't done since the death of my grandmother three years earlier. She attempted to console me as best she could, explaining that I was not really healthy enough to play anyway. However, at 13 years old, I couldn't associate being cut from the team with my injured ankle. All I could grasp was that this meant Coach Barfield was saying "I'm not good enough."

"Our most honest reveal is in how we respond to criticism and challenge, not how we accept praise or navigate in comfort!"

This poured fuel on a fire that burned passionately for the remainder of my football career, and in everyday life today. I set out to prove Coach Barfield wrong, and anyone else who ever doubted me. One of my middle school teachers recently shared with me that when she and other teachers questioned Coach Barfield about cutting me from the team, he actually shared with them that he felt I had a bright future ahead of me in football if I so choose, so he wasn't going to risk it for me to play middle-school football. So the nurturing by design was at work even when I felt at the time I was being stymied. A presumably negative experience in my life served as an additional catalyst for great accomplishments. So character was discovered in the response. Our most honest reveal is in how we respond to criticism and challenge, not how we accept praise or navigate in comfort!

I was never the same on the football field. Though I hadn't completely grasped what it took to be an elite player at that point, the tenacious disposition was permanently entrenched. Also, blazoned around my left ankle was an appropriately symbolic reminder of what ignited the flame. I wear the scar as a badge of honor, for without the trial, I don't know that I would have the same appreciation for the triumph. As the years passed, this drive was nurtured and properly directed in a manner that catapulted me all the way to the pinnacle of a sport which had once told the 8th Grade me "I wasn't good enough."

"I wear this scar as a badge of honor, for without the trial, I don't know that I would have the same appreciation for the triumph."

My professional football experience was particularly wrought with similar lessons. During my NFL career I persevered through a knee reconstruction (ACL, MCL, and meniscus), a broken leg, many ankle sprains, chronic hamstring pulls, several (unreported) concussions, and, finally, a herniated cervical disc with fractures to my C5 & C6 vertebrae that forced me to retire.

Unfortunately, I suffered that knee injury during only my second year in the league. Prior to that setback I had prototypical instincts, athleticism, speed, and explosiveness, to go along with my unique frame at 6 feet 3 inches, 215 pounds. Heading into the 1993 NFL draft I had some of the best college production and measurable attributes for success at the safety position.

Respected talent evaluator Ron Wolf, who was the Green Bay Packers' General Manager at the time, issued the following resounding quote:

"Tim Watson is a strong safety from Howard who is probably the best—this is probably a very strong statement—but he is probably the best tackler in the draft. Watson is a unique case. He is just a tremendous tackler. And it's something we needed to add to our football team—another tough guy back in there. And he's a tough man . . . a tough man."

But choosing to go to Howard University instead of a football powerhouse was enough to raise doubts, or at least provide excuses. I was only a 6th Round draft choice (selection #156). There were a lot of questions about what type of player I could be on the professional level. That is until I got on the football fields in the NFL and proved to be quite the talent. So much so that just prior to my knee injury I had taken over the starting strong safety duties going into the first game of the 1994 season. My agent was actually in early discussions with the Chiefs on a contract extension with a considerable signing bonus and salary increase. However, wouldn't you know that the career changing play occurred on the season-opening kickoff and I never got to enjoy the fruits of the labor that had earned me that starting job. So I never, during my football career, received anything close to the millions of dollars earned by many NFL players today. As a matter of fact, my post-football career has been much more financially rewarding. My signing bonus in 1993 was $36,000. The salaries that followed for the next four years were $100,000; $135,000; $178,000; and $215,000 respectively. Besides my $68,000.00 share of playoff money during my rookie year—in which I was able to enjoy a trip with the Kansas City Chiefs to the AFC Championship game—that signing bonus was the largest single check that I received. Comparatively, each year there were a number of my teammates whose weekly checks exceeded my entire annual salary. This gave me even more perspective and appreciation for the values instilled by my parents and other mentors. Those checks would never be able to define the value of who I am. The tenacity that I displayed on the field also needed to be consistent throughout my life. So, my formal education and REALS were always supremely important. It was a must for me to cultivate excellence in all of my talents. Football was just a temporary path of a long journey.

"One of the greatest benefits of life here on earth is its provision of a constant classroom, and thankfully I'm a voluntary perpetual learner."

One of the greatest benefits of life here on earth is its provision of a constant classroom, and thankfully I'm a voluntary perpetual learner. However, there's a bit of irony in the classroom of life. Comfort and convenience are never the prime ingredients for growth or maturity. We are more likely to appreciate the great times when we've experienced the tough times. Interestingly when many people hear my story for the first time, they think sympathy is in order for how my NFL career played out. However, I quickly share with them that I was able to live out a dream millions of others never will. I can appreciate everything about my experiences in the NFL, and remained thankful and joyful the entire time. True joy in life is based in contentment, not achievement. Displays of emotion like happiness, sadness, and anger are external reflections of our feelings toward external conditions. Of course in my fallible humanity, I've experienced all these emotions. However, I'm blessed with a full understanding that my internal joy is not subject to such constraints.

And for an even greater sense of perspective, at the time I retired in 1999 a startling statistic was shared with me: Out of the 15,018 men that had played in the NFL over the previous 20 years, only 631 played for three years or more. I am one of them. See, just as was the case in my middle school football experience, even presumed failure has its place. We must truly listen as God speaks through the depths of our hearts. For human intent will never trump God's purpose! Often, we will find the greatest opportunities for personal maturity in our disappointments. For me there were much grander plans beyond the football field.

April 27, 1993

Tim Watson
1409 Monroe Street NE
Washington, DC 20017

Player's Representative:
Tony Agnone
Eastern Athletic Services
9515 Deereco Rd., Ste. 710
Timonium, MD 21093

Drafting Club:
GREEN BAY PACKERS
1265 Lombardi Avenue
Green Bay, WI 54304

Dear Tim:

This letter serves as notice that you have been selected by the Green Bay Packers of the National Football League in the Annual Selection Meeting.

In selecting you, the Green Bay Packers have tendered to you a one-year NFL Player Contract for the 1993 Minimum Active/Inactive List salary of $100,000.

You or your representative may contact Mike Reinfeldt, Chief Financial Officer of the Green Bay Packers to receive further information.

Sincerely,

RONALD M. WOLF
Executive Vice President/General Manager

RW/rgt

1993 NFL Draft Selection Letter

"Comfort and convenience are never the prime ingredients for growth or maturity."

We all will be faced with ups and downs . . . . elation and trials . . . smiles and frowns. My life has been productive, but not perfect. Like the Apostle Paul I've had plenty, and at times been without. Likewise, I've been able to maintain persistent joy not subject to my changing circumstances. This came by the realization of purpose, and contentment driven by my thematic biblical principle of Phil 4:13 *"I can endure all things with Jesus Christ who provides me strength."* For anyone who's ever received my autograph, this verse should be familiar.

I realize that the road to my life's success is most certainly paved for a plan that is bigger than I. My mentors groomed me through solid relationships and deliberate processes. We realized together that life's ups and downs are never about any one person individually. Each of our experiences (both positive and negative) is a resource for UPLIFTing those with whom we have the honor of sharing life and wisdom.

"We must all commit to a systematic delivery of exceptional conditioning of our minds, bodies, and spirits in order to truly live exceptionally."

A fortunate ancillary benefit for me has been the fact that the "tools" provided here have made an immeasurable impact on my own life. Again, the ability to achieve success is available to anyone willing to proactively cultivate it. What I am sharing are some easily referenced systems and principles I formulated to remain accountable to my plan for success. I also use some words in a different way that will hopefully help provide a positive paradigm shift. We must all commit to a systematic delivery of exceptional conditioning of our minds, bodies, and spirits in order to truly live exceptionally. My desire is for you to get away from the usual ordinary approaches to life and experience the extraordinary.

Philadelphia Eagles—1997

SECTION II:

COMMUNICATING OUR CORE

Chapter 5

 The Iceberg Principle

Core character components are cultivated during our formative years. They are products of our nurturing from both deliberate and unplanned influences. Multiple elements are developed, but they are often not recognizable by others. An Iceberg serves as an excellent analogy of this phenomenon: Character is internally formed (subconsciously existent) in full, but oftentimes externally portrayed (consciously displayed) in small parts. As with icebergs, approximately 90% of what defines us is below the surface. In our subconscious rests these nurtured influences to our conscious behaviors and accomplishments:

- Knowledge—both formally acquired intellect, and experientially acquired wisdom

- Inspirations—things that motivate us to do what we do
- Values—our moral code and/or spiritual belief system
- Talents—special natural abilities or aptitudes; a predisposed superior quality capable of relative achievement or success
- Attitude—a positive or negative mental disposition towards a particular person, place, thing, or action

All of these items influence our observable behaviors and measurable accomplishments. Although these external expressions are only 10% of who we are, they're all others will have to develop a perception of us. Because circumstances are subject to change without warning, we are also subject to uncharacteristic reactions to them. When our reaction is unpleasant, this could be misconstrued as an internal character flaw rather than being attributed to the circumstances. In social psychology this is called *the fundamental attribution error.*

We don't live in a world where our behaviors are often allowed the luxury of explanation by social psychological theories, and even more importantly, we never get a second chance to make a first impression. Ray Kroc, the founder of McDonald's Restaurants, said "The quality of individuals is reflected in the standards that they set for themselves." For subscribers to this idea it's very important that the relatively small outer representation of our core be an accurate reflection. A proactive approach is necessary to insure that it is. Our best representation is consistent behavior (both proactive and reactive) that positively and accurately reflects our character.

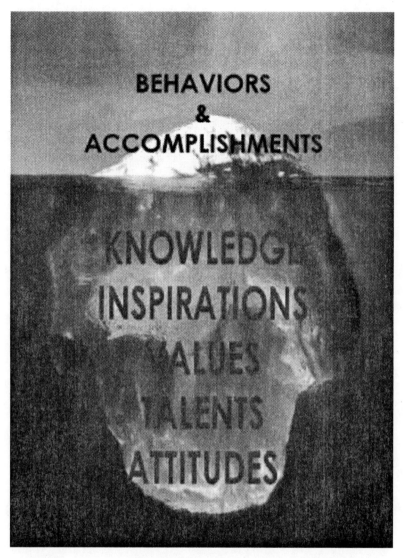

The Iceberg Principle

"The quality of individuals is reflected in the standards that they set for themselves."
-Ray Kroc, founder of McDonald's

The reason most people can easily recognize and associate logo images and slogans with companies like McDonalds, State Farm Insurance, and the National Football League is because each has built an extremely effective brand. We should all take heed of their commercial genius, and do the same for ourselves personally. In our everyday lives, the world's opinion of who we are and what we represent indicates our choice of personal brand. This holds true for each and every one of us. So to the outside world we are not necessarily perceived as who/what we say we are, but who/what we demonstrate ourselves to be. What do you want the world to see in you?

Regardless of what career we choose, presenting an attractive image is important. Everyone has some degree of dependency on others, both personally and professionally. These people are more likely to be positive advocates within our spheres of influence when we are also perceived positively. We do have a degree of control over the way this perception is formulated. The personal image we project most often through our words and deeds will be who or what people see us to be. So it's up to us to condition ourselves to behave in a manner reflective of our admirable character traits. Here's how to tell whether or not we are effectively reflecting positive personal brands:

- **Consistency**—Behaviors and accomplishments must be steady.
- **Value**—We must be valuable to others (be a giver, not just a taker).
- **Authenticity**—We need to bring unique ideas and talents; we should not just replicate other people and dated ideologies.
- **Positive Engagement**—We should be positively engaging. Be enthusiastic, with refreshing energy that exudes optimism. In communicating, we want to be a "shuttle launch" that attracts constructive interest, and not a "train wreck" drawing morbid curiosity.
- **Deliver On Our Promises**—We must be reliable, following through on commitments to completion. In other words, we must "Live our Creed."

We live in an age of modern technology with virtual and digital communication mediums advancing daily. In addition to usual media, most of us have access to social media networks; along with virtual meetings, interviews, presentations, and even dating. It's highly likely that our reputations (personal brands) will precede our personal introductions to potential business or personal associates. Prudency would suggest we build a consistent, valuable, authentic, positively engaging, and reliable reputation regardless of the medium of communication. We are on display even when we're unaware, so we should make sure we're displaying an attractive authentic brand.

The Value of our Attitudes

Chapter 6

```
┌─────────────────────────────────────────┐
│                                         │
│  UPLIFT                                 │
│  POSIVITY                               │
│  R.E.A.P. what you S.O.E.™              │
│                                         │
└─────────────────────────────────────────┘
```

The Royal Treatment™

Approximately five years ago I had the good fortune to meet one of the most well branded business associates I've ever known. An incident that started out as a negative one for me was turned into a lesson in the power of a positive attitude. The purveyor was a local credit union manager named Kathy Royal. Prior to our meeting I had made numerous unsuccessful attempts online and via phone to have some monthly bills set up on their automatic bill paying system. Finally exasperated with presumably poor service, I headed down to the local branch early one morning determined to give them a piece of my mind. As I drove the relatively short trip my anger grew. I went over and over in my head the choice words I would have for whomever dared ask "May I help you?"

"On this day God saw fit to send me the person with the happiest disposition I have ever experienced in my life."

Upon my arrival inside the bank I was greeted with a warm smile from the receptionist. I quickly disposed of her warmth with a very matter of fact *"I need to see your manager now!"* On this day God saw fit to send me the person with the happiest disposition I have ever experienced in my life. The receptionist proceeded to retrieve the manager, and out walks Ms. Royal. Finally calm enough to not make a scene in the lobby, I extended my hand to accept the firm handshake that accompanied her huge smile. As we spoke briefly during the walk to her office I could sense in her uncommonly chipper tone that my attempt at anger was in for a battle. Well the fight was over as soon as she closed the door behind me and asked me to have a seat. There was nothing I could say to remove her smile or change her positive attitude. And believe me I tried. As a matter of fact, she became even more upbeat and cheerful as time passed. All the while she was taking care of the problem for which I journeyed there. Before I knew what hit me, my accounts were set up properly, and I actually began responding to Ms. Royal in the same pleasant manner in which she addressed me.

I came to discover in short order that Ms. Royal was also a believer in Jesus Christ. So, the Source of her joy was really no mystery. However, she did a great job of letting Christ's light shine through her. The rays certainly shined on me that day, and she remained consistent in all our future contacts. For the remainder of my business relationship with that credit union I never dealt with anyone except Ms. Royal. I also recommended her to everyone I knew in the area. Now, in training sessions and with my speaking audiences, I often share this experience. Her over-the-top positivity is dubbed ***The Royal Treatment***™. Her brand is undeniable: She has consistently and authentically delivered value as "the extremely positive banker who's happy to serve you." I've found her attitude particularly inspiring and useable in both business and personal interactions.

Chapter 7

" Talking White"

My personal experience with the ***Iceberg Principle***™ was both humbling and rewarding. I remember a time when I certainly was not exhibiting outwardly what I had been developing inwardly. We all probably have a number of things in our childhoods that give us a good laugh. I'm no different than anyone else in that regard. However, there was one aspect of my childhood that provided youthful humor, but was a rude awakening for me as a young adult.

Often when a news story breaks in one of America's small towns or inner-city neighborhoods it seems that the roving reporter somehow finds the most inarticulate person on the scene to interview. Additionally, this person will often be wearing some form of garb that is unsuitable for public appearances. These spectacles have become comic relief for YouTube, web blogs, and late night talk shows. We "educated" and "enlightened" people tend to lead the laughing parades. Is there anyone besides me who finds a bit of hypocrisy in our finding fodder in this?

I was very present during the birth and growth of Hip-Hop culture. We would often make fun of kids (particularly minorities) who spoke correct English via a standard dialect. My group of friends poignantly referred to it as "talking white." It was not viewed as cool to "talk white". Culturally, we found a way to justify our "cool" dialect by taking ownership of it and titling it "Ebonics." I'm proud to be a member of the first generation in this country to really enjoy the freedoms for which many of our grandparents and parents fought and died. So I understand the pride in ownership we took creating a new and contagious culture. However, we failed to realize that the primary building blocks for our dialect were grammatical and literary ignorance. This ignorance was grounded in the inferior educational systems in which many of our pioneers were schooled. We are certainly a creative people who found a way to communicate effectively with one another and call it "cool." Somewhere along the way, however, we missed what the fighting and dying was all about: the equal right to vote, to jobs, to public transportation, to housing, to economic empowerment, and to a quality education. Upon acquiring access to quality education in a country where the predominant and official language is English, it would behoove those motivated toward progress to learn to use it properly in both spoken and written communications. That's the only way anyone will be able to effectively share what he has cultivated internally with a diverse audience.

I had friends who spoke proper English when we were growing up in tiny Fort Valley. Unfortunately though, they were few, and I for the most part was not one of them. One was Alecia Johnson (now Alecia Johnson-Livatt). This young lady in my graduating class had proper English down to a science. Both her casual everyday speech and formal presentations were extraordinary. One day in eighth grade our homeroom teacher Mrs. Robinson shared an observation that showed the conscious mastery of English Alecia displayed. Alecia consistently approached female teachers with their proper honorific, addressing married teachers with the appropriate Mrs. and unmarried ones with Miss. Many of the rest of us were still struggling with dangling participles and ending sentences in prepositions. So for us the customary Ms. was universally applied. Years later I had the occasion to share with Alecia how impressed I was with her communication skills. By that time, of course, I had myself discovered the importance of this conditioned ability on effective core communications. When this subject has come up in conversation with people from my hometown, one of the excuses bantered about is that we were just "country," and our inner city comrades were just "ghetto." Well, Alecia Johnson-Livatt was raised and educated in the same "country" environment as the rest of us. However, her "light switch" was obviously flipped on earlier to condition herself as she did. Many of us kids were missing both skill and will in this conundrum. We weren't trained to speak properly, nor were we even attempting it.

Thankfully, my skill and will were both rudely awakened when a college professor of mine finally showed me that she really cared. She challenged me to speak in a manner that matched my intellect as demonstrated through my grades. Initially I was upset at her for embarrassing me. I thought "how dare she call me out when I get better grades than most of the other students in the class." However, I began to see the absurdity of how I sounded when she had me record and listen to myself speak. This went on for many months before I displayed a noticeable improvement. I then enrolled in a speech class and began developing presentation skills along with better speaking habits. This served as a catalyst for cultivating a new and rewarding talent that allowed me to effectively share my passions with others. It didn't happen overnight for me, but I began to write and practice speeches. Later I began filming myself to critique my grammar, dialect, and delivery. Through proper conditioning, the skill has grown to the degree that today I am a well respected professional public speaker.

This transformation gives me relativity, perspective, and appreciation. I can relate to the people being interviewed on television, and served up as America's headline jokes. I can understand the origin of their communication skills. But I can also appreciate that improper speech is really NOT a laughing matter. Those of us who have been educated and enlightened beyond our ignorance should go back into the small town/inner-city neighborhoods and schools to help mentor the next generation. That way they will be able to have relativity, perspective, and an appreciation of us.

On my personal Iceberg, one of my behaviors (poor speech) provided an inaccurate view of its relative component within my core (an impressive intellect). Thankfully, a humbling discovery resulted in a rewarding development that allowed me to release the stigma of "talking white" and become proud of the skill of speaking English correctly!

SECTION III:

OMPLEMENTARY COMPANIONS

Chapter 8

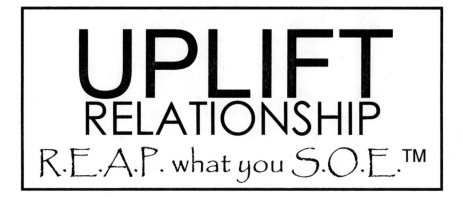

Influential Acquaintance

As previously shared, relationships have been the foundation of my journey. I've had ones that brought me sorrow, and many have produced great joy. There have been those who attempted to hold me down, and numerous who've helped catapult me to the top. I've enjoyed relationships with many casual acquaintances, and several lifelong friends. My heart has been broken by lost love, and filled with the love I've found. Each of these relationships, whether fleeting or enduring, has been crucial to who I am today. Foundational relationships are the primary building blocks for anyone to cultivate success in any area of life.

Our acquaintances come in and out of our lives through varying degrees of interpersonal connection. It may be for a specific purpose, a finite stage, or a lifetime. The specific purpose of a relationship might be to meet a stated or implied need. Once the need is met, the relationship is over. It's important for us to know when that time has come. Because attempting to draw from a relationship beyond its intended purpose usually leads to stagnation. Neither person is growing during this time. We must all know when to say when!

The stages we go through in life will vary in length. So will the relationships with people who experience them along with us. The completion of specific phases will also coincide with the ending of some relationships. In these circumstances the culmination of the relationship is needed in order that we might move on to additional purposes and stages of our lives. The ascending levels of our development occur during ascending stages of our lives.

Lifetime relationships are those connections to which we commit a lifetime of cultivation. We will usually experienced our deepest connections with those people whom we share the most experiences. This type of relationship endures the ups and downs of life without severing the connection. Lifetime relationships will travel across all the phases and purposes of our lives. It's important to our emotional well being to have the correct type of acquaintance within this category. The caveat is to actually know the distinction between mere companions, and a trusting reciprocally beneficial relationship. The fact is everyone is not in our corner to help us succeed, or comfort us when we fail. Some are there just because, and only when, we are deemed successful. And there are even some waiting in the rafters for us to struggle in order to feel good about themselves. So the key is just to be wise in making the distinction of who really encompasses our lifelong inner circles. That's a place where only family and friendship should dwell! I've learned this the hard way at times in my own life. Having experience in the lows of financial struggle, while also having been to the purported mountaintop of financial success, I've seen the reveal first hand. There have been those who I thought were my friends who disappeared after the notoriety and accoutrements of the NFL seemed to wane. Within this same group were people whom I called upon when I needed assistance who suddenly dodged my phone calls. But, fortunately there were also true friends who oftentimes offered assistance, comfort, or support even when unsolicited. Never confuse comrades with friends. In times of trial only one of the two will lend a genuine helping hand!

Throughout our lives there will be a number of people in each of the three categories. Foundational relationships will be formed in each as well. These are defined by evident reciprocal influence by each of the parties. The value of any relationship, regardless of its depth or breadth, can be measured by the influence it has on our lives:

1. **Neutral Effect**—little to no influence on our behavior
2. **Degrading Effect**—negative influence on our behavior
3. **Productive Effect**—positive influence on our behavior

"He who walks with the wise grows wise; but a companion of fools suffers harm."
-Proverbs 13:20

Foundational relationships will come in the forms of both degrading and productive Effects. The obvious ideal types to help cultivate our success are productive. This desired reciprocal influence can be best described as positive relativity. A great biblical reference is found in Proverbs 13:20—*"He who walks with the wise grows wise; but a companion of fools suffers harm."* Productive relationships will provide reciprocal positive growth. Conversely, negative relationships will provide reciprocal detriment. Strong consideration should be given to this counsel prior to forming any associations. Before beginning new relationships we should first discern the person's/group's complementary and contradictory character traits relative to our own. This will serve as an excellent gauge for choosing people with whom we should associate. Then our relationships can be best cultivated to fruitful maturity. We should all take a closer look at the company we keep, and evaluate whether or not there's wisdom to be gained.

Many express disbelief at the news of immoral/illegal activities by certain people they knew growing up: those now living an X minus life. I contend that this result is no surprise at all. Those suffering disbelief probably neglected to observe the relationships these individuals made during their formative years. If we are really interested in knowing how the direction we're heading in life is perceived then we need look no further than our five closest friends. They are reflections of us more than we consciously know. We must make sure that those closest to us share our core values, and compliment our ambitions. Relationships should always be reciprocal. In order for us to have lifelong development we also need people in our lives who challenge us to grow. We should avoid those just along for the ride. It's also a decent idea to not be the smartest, wealthiest, or most successful person in your group of friends. Though you might enjoy the ego boost from being either of these, your growth will be stagnant.

"If we are really interested in knowing how the direction we're heading in life is perceived then we need look no further than our five closest friends."

"To thy own self be true . . . And it must follow, as the night the day. Thou cannot then be false to any man." This Shakespeare quote from Hamlet speaks profoundly on reflecting ourselves genuinely and positively. The process starts with you! The predominant *"Law of Attraction"* in forming close relationships is *we attract that which we project.* Before we are able to accurately project our core we need to make sure we are cognizant of it. There are times in life we find ourselves in urgent situations making important decisions. If we haven't previously come to a conscious understanding of what we truly believe about the subject matter, it's likely the sense of urgency will drive our decision rather than our core beliefs.

Self-Awareness is an important key to our contentment. Values and lifestyle are choices that we should be sure to appropriately align with who we are. I admit that I'm attracted to confident people who are NOT OK with *"just getting by."* Would've, could've, and should've aren't in my lingo, and ordinary just doesn't do it for me! I'm going to enjoy the best God allows for me in this life, and GO HARD until the *wheels fall off!* I also know that it's important for me to surround myself with other people who approach life similarly.

I've designed a tool to help with self-discovery of our value systems, along with sharing who we are with others. Please take a moment to answer the questions in the ACCT Profile (Acquaintance Character Compatibility Test) at the end of this chapter. Also, make a copy for your five closest friends and have them complete the form as well. There are very personal reveals within this assessment. Only exchange the results with those friends who you trust most and with whom you wish to build the strongest relationships. All will find this exercise enlightening personally and comparatively. The most important result of this exercise is your self-analysis. However, almost as relevant will be who you choose to view your results—who you really view as friends. Without trust, there is no friendship.

ACCT Profile™
Acquaintance Character Compatibility Test
For accurate compatibility answer all questions factually as you are; not the way you would like to be.

1. What is your full given name and nickname(s) if any?

   (a) Full Name: _____
   (b) Nickname(s): _____

2. What is your birth date? _____

3. (a) Where were you born? _____
   (b) Where do you live now? _____

4. (a) How many siblings do you have? _____
   (b) List their ages and respective names: _____

5. What was the makeup of your juvenile guardianship?
   A. Married Parents
   B. Unmarried Parents
   C. Single Parent
   D. Divorced Parents
   E. Foster Home/Homes

6. During your youth what did you aspire
   to be as an adult? _____

7. (a) What high school did you attend
   and did you finish? _____
   (b) What was your Grade Point Average? _____

8. (a) What college did you attend and
   did you finish? _____
   (b) What was your Grade Point Average? _____
   (c) What was your College Major? _____
   (d) What degree(s) have you earned? _____
      A. Associates
      B. Bachelors

    C. Post-Graduate
    D. Masters
    E. Doctorate

9. What is your current profession; who's your employer; and what position do you hold with the company?

    _____

10. (a) What is your annual household income?
    A. Below $63,700
    B. $63,701—$128,500
    C. $128,501—$195,850
    D. $195,850—$349,700
    E. Over $349,700

(b) How would you describe your spending habits? _____
    A. Very Frugal
    B. Moderate Lifestyle
    C. Enjoy the Finer Things

(c) What is your highest credit score? _____

(d) Have you ever filed for bankruptcy protection?
    A. Yes
    B. No

11. What is your relationship status?
    A. Single
    B. In Relationship, Partner's Name:_____
    C. Married, Spouse's Name: _____

12. What is your sexual orientation?
    A. Heterosexual
    B. Homosexual
    C. Bisexual

13. What is your stance on premarital sex?
    A. OK with protection

    B. Abstinence is best
    C. OK in a committed relationship

14. What is your stance on Homosexual Marriages/Relationships?
    A. For, Elaborate: _____
    B. Against, Elaborate: _____
    C. Neutral, Elaborate: _____

15. How do you feel about interethnic friendships, dating, and marriages?
    A. For, Elaborate: _____
    B. Against, Elaborate: _____
    C. Neutral, Elaborate: _____

16. Do you personally have interethnic friendships?
    A. Yes
    B. No

17. What is your religious affiliation?
    A. Christian __ Catholic __ Orthodox __ Protestant
    B. Islam __ Shiite Muslims __ Sunni Muslims
    C. __ Black Muslims
    D. Judaism __Orthodox __Conservative __Reform
    E. __Messianic
    F. Hinduism
    G. Buddhism
    H. Other _____

18. What is your position on abortion?
    S. Pro-Choice, Elaborate: _____
    U. Anti-Abortion, Elaborate: _____
    W. Pro-Abortion, Elaborate: _____

19. What is your position on the death penalty?
    T. For, Elaborate: _____
    U. Against, Elaborate: _____

20. (a) Do you have children?

A. Yes
B. No

(b) If not, would you like to have children?
A. Yes
B. No

(c) If yes, how many children do you have? _____

(d) List their ages and respective names: _____

21. (a) Do you drink alcoholic beverages?
A. Yes, often.
B. Yes, but rarely.
C. No

(b) Do you smoke cigarettes?
A. Yes
B. No

22. (a) Do you regularly use swear words?
A. Yes
B. No

(b) Do you allow your children to use swear words?
A. Yes
B. No

23. How do you feel about corporal punishment?
X. For, Elaborate: _____
Y. Against, Elaborate: _____

24. What is your political affinity or affiliation?
A. Democratic
B. Republican
C. Independent
D. Other: _____

25. What would be the makeup of your ideal neighborhood?
A. Exclusive to your ethnicity/culture
B. Ethnically/Culturally Diverse
C. Majority Caucasian

D. Majority Minority

26. Number from 1-12 by order of importance the following elements as they prioritize in your life with 1 representing what is most important:

    (a)___Work/Life Balance (e)___Money/Wealth (i)___Integrity
    (b)___Faith/Religion (f)___Health/Fitness (j)_____Status
    (c)___Commitment (g)___Fun/Leisure (k)___Passion
    (d)___Honesty (h)___Family/Friends (l)___Diversity

27. What is your stance on War?
    A. For
    B. Against
    C. Neutral

28. Do you support any charitable causes/organizations?
    A. Yes, Financially
    B. Yes, through Volunteerism/Service
    C. No

29. What are your interests/hobbies? _____
    _____
    _____

30. (a) Are you a member of a religious organization/church?
    _____

    (b) If yes, what is the name of the organization/church?
    _____

31. (a) Are you a member of any civic or fraternal organizations?
    _____

    (b) If yes, what is the name of the organization(s)?
    _____

32. If you have taken the quadrant styled personality test, what was your result? If you haven't taken the test, select the category(s)

that best describe your style of behavior. If you fit into more than one category, list them in ascending order with the first one being your most dominant style:

A. Analytical—systematic, organized, and logical.
B. Driver—decisive, assertive, risk taker.
C. Amiable—empathetic, considerate, and easygoing.
D. Expressive—outgoing, enthusiastic, and animated.

33. Besides the recipient of this profile, list your three closest friends:

- _____
- _____
- _____

Chapter 9

$\mathscr{F}$riendship is Essential to the Soul

One of the most important components of our success will be our choices and management of friendships. Though we'll have varying degrees of connection with different people, friendship is the most productive objective. Our challenge is to choose who exactly merits that distinction, because people are around us for many different reasons. A great place to start is gauging their presence during your storms. Failure seems to constantly travel alone. But success always has company. Think of the times you've done things wrong or made mistakes. Did many others line up to take the blame for it? Now think of the times you've had great accomplishments. How many people were ready and willing to share the credit? It's no coincidence that most celebrities have entourages, yet hobos we see on the streets are usually alone. This is a selectivity we human beings have within us. Success, whether perceived or actual, is naturally attractive. Conversely, struggle is unattractive. That's why we must be selective in our choices of friends—not by judging others, but by discerning values and traits consistent with ours. There is nothing wrong with having differences with your acquaintances. However, they should be complementary, not contradictory. Those who complement us do so also during our struggles.

"Failure seems to constantly travel alone. But success always has company."

Many people misuse the title of friend. It is the person who sits next to us at work, the people who call only when they need something, the person who tells us everything we want to hear, and even the guy we just met marching in a picket line. Because it encompasses love, trust, honesty, altruism, loyalty, empathy, and truth, I'm suggesting that friendship deserves more respect than that. Let's be loving, trusting, honest, altruistic, loyal, empathetic, and truthful. Our real friends will reflect the same. If you truly want to know who your friends are, evaluate the times your acquaintances were aware of forthcoming demanding tasks, or troubling news of yours. What were the responses? Who carried on indifferently? Who offered unsolicited help or shared empathetic conversation? When you're in need, you don't have to ask your true friends for help. Nor will they ask if you need their help. They just help! You'll know them by their works, not their words. The greatest feeling in the world is knowing you have special people who care. These are our friends!

"Let's be loving, trusting, honest, altruistic, loyal, empathetic, and truthful. Our real friends will reflect the same."

Friendship

49

SECTION IV:

OVE ALLIANCES

Chapter 10

$\mathscr{R}$omance: Finding Mr. or Mrs. Right

Romantic relationships are certainly one of the most complex commitments. They are also high risk/ high reward undertakings spiritually, mentally, emotionally, and even physically. Exposing ourselves requires that we take the vetting process for compatibility even more seriously than we do with friends. When you find someone you deem a suitable candidate for your love, you should exchange the ACCT Profile with them, or ask very similar questions during the discovery process. For me there is certainly nothing more personal being shared in the ACCT Profile than my heart. My wife and I did this very early on in our relationship and found great compatibility.

Romantic relationships can be put in the same categories as any other. So, we become romantically involved to fulfill specific needs, and/or within a particular phase of our lives with someone who is complementary to us, and possibly with a love connection that lasts a lifetime. Additionally, our romantic partner might have little or no influence, a negative influence, or a positive influence on us. Because of the transparency and emotional vulnerability within these relationships, they are the most important interpersonal connections we'll experience during our lives. Thus, the most influence on your behavior will come from these relationships.

I've experienced my share of the heartaches and joys of romantic relationships. I've caused some of both as well. Through these experiences I've been able to grow immensely. There were mistakes that I made, from which I've become a better man. I've learned how a woman should be treated. At the same time I uncovered my own mysteries. There were things I didn't know I needed to have in the right woman for me. This chapter shares those discoveries, and how they might be useful in your love life as well.

Especially after a bad relationship outcome, many people are unfortunately looking outside of themselves for the contentment that's needed to attract the right person, when the fact is you have to be the right person to attract whom you desire. When it's right both people will make every effort to be who they should be, both for themselves and for their mate. That is what creates the autonomous joy upon which good or bad circumstances have no effect. The relationship stands solidly and with sovereignty!

I understand pessimism following breakups. However, I want to also share with you the reason for my hope. It appears to me that many of you who are either divorced or have had a bad break-up are now suffering from "buyer's remorse" from having experienced a "lemon." Having had a failed marriage or other serious relationship is one of the biggest voids of the heart, so you are now probably approaching prospects with one of a couple of skewed views:

1. **The desire to be wanted and loved is so strong that you end up "tolerating" less than what you deserve because it sometimes feels good; or**

2. **You are overly cautious and place unrealistic expectations on all potential suitors to ensure you never again suffer the wrongs you endured in the failed relationship.**

Believe me, I understand and empathize with these views. I just still believed the real ONE was available to me. There are two reasons I had hope:

1. **God has never failed me and He certainly didn't in this either (however, He has taught me lessons along the journey).**
2. **I'm being the RIGHT ONE for the RIGHT ONE and we've BECOME ONE!**

Don't search—just be you and he/she will find you! Being is not about becoming a recluse . . . you need to present your manhood or womanhood in the right forums. Make sure though that your inner world is calm. We are unable to make clear choices in times of storm. Be at peace with yourself, and he/she will find you.

We were not "designed" to be alone. But, I don't judge those who've developed the ability to go solo. My personal "balance" comes with a lady on my arm. So, I'm 100% in favor of not letting oneself grow indifferent to wanting or feeling wanted.

Romantic connections have many ingredients: physical, emotional, spiritual, and intellectual. I personally enjoy "nice things" and "nice looking things." But the most attractive female attributes to me are Christ-centered spirituality, altruism, intellect, sensuality, and class. It is great when they all come together in the same package. But this discovery takes patience and a willing effort from both parties. No more settling for me. I've been patient through bad choices, and I'm now willing to put in the effort with a great one. It's my privilege to make sure that I'm everything she wants in a man, and she IS reciprocating!

We each have but one life and we shouldn't spend a moment of it in love relationships with immature boys or girls. There are men and women who will view their time as more precious when spent with us. My friends, if he/she does not delight in your presence, then he/she doesn't deserve your company—much less your heart. If he/she's not proud to step out with you, then tell him/her to "get to stepping." You value you and the right man/woman will, too! We are certainly not to gauge our happiness on the behavior of another towards us. However, there is absolutely nothing wrong with enjoying and sharing life with the right person.

Oneness is Key

For a relationship to thrive, there are some essential components that will not fit into the "options" category. These necessities include shared FAITH, genuine LOVE, mutual RESPECT, enduring FAITHFULNESS, active ALTRUISM, considerate HONESTY, absolute FORGIVENESS, consistent INTEGRITY, unwavering LOYALTY, and reliable TRUST. This trust is a wonderful gift. It reflects a belief in the mutuality of all the other essentials. This mutuality is the essence of success. When his concern is not focused on himself, but on pleasing her . . . and she's reciprocating the same, then neither is left wanting. Trustworthiness is an extremely heavy responsibility. Be deliberate in choosing from whom you expect such accountability and consistency of character. Especially be sure that you have the strength to bear the load yourself. Temptation is always accompanied by choice . . . choosing wisely in calm moments makes for superior handling of the storms! Fortunate are those who choose well, and thereby find Mr. or Mrs. RIGHT!

Chapter 11

*W*hat is love?

Shared within the Bible in 1 John 4:16 is "*And we have come to know and have believed the love which God has for us. God is love, and the one who abides in love abides in God, and God abides in him.*" So if we want to know love then we need to know God. Also, the Apostle Paul addressed love to the Corinthians of biblical times throughout letters to the early believers in the ministry of Jesus Christ. In the original Greek language he shared God's message on agape (biblically used to denote affection born from an internal sense of value of the person being loved), storge (natural affection that occurs within families, such as the case of parents and their children), and philia (fondness developed as mankind builds relationships and recognizes commonalities). The other context used to denote love, eros (romantic attractive or arousal), was widely referenced in Greek culture in biblical times; but never was it mentioned in the Bible even once. The phrase "love is a verb" has become a bit cliché, but Paul wrote some poignant and powerful words that back the saying as truth. The noun philia, the most common word for love used by Greeks during the times, is only found once in the Bible. However, the verb phileo occurs twenty-five(25) times. More so, agape (which was least used in the Greek culture of ancient times), was used in its various forms three-hundred-twenty(320) times throughout the New Testament. Today agape is often referenced as "unconditional love." There were professions of love being patient and kind; and that it always (not sometimes) protects, trusts, hopes, and perseveres. Most importantly proclaimed was that "**love never fails!**"

Unfortunately, many people within romantic relationships only experience eros, and never ascend to a philia level connection of any real substance. Storge often finds its most transparent reveal when we ourselves become parents, which of course not everyone experiences. But very rarely does man ever even understand the expression of agape as is biblically referenced. So, many of us unfortunately have a misappropriated label on the affections we experience in this life. When we go through relationships that fail and we assert that we "fell out of love," we are contradicting truth. The reality is that if we "Fall out of love" then we were never in it! We must stop confusing our lusts and likes with God's love! Developing a true philia type connection is necessary to discovering commonalities that bond us beyond the superficial. At the ideal ascension to agape, we are able to love in spite of everything, not because of anything. The key is whether or not a relationship is ever cultivated to the actual development of ascension in love. If so the love will never cease, even if the romantic attraction fails. That's why the marital union is designed to be between one man and one woman. If we actually develop true love for more than one person, then we'd better be prepared to deal with its lingering emotional presence for the entirety of our lives. I'm of the opinion that this scenario very rarely happens, if at all. Instead, I believe, as previously mentioned, that we mistake our eros inspired lusts and likes for His love. These emotions don't endure the "storms" of life.

In application, eros attraction is just one aspect of a marriage or other romantic relationship in which two people profess "love" for each other.

Many of the complementary traits of the couple are formed through the bonding within philia. Ultimately, this is the most important contextual application of love between humans within marriages, or failure is certain to occur. Agape is the icing on the cake. But we aren't to fool ourselves into thinking in our fallibility that we can enjoy this "unconditional" level of connection without having intentionally grown together through some common attraction of philia love. Paul was definitive in the attribute of real love's endurance. However, through many of our relationships, we more than likely unfortunately never venture beyond the eros connection.

Our biggest quandary in love is probably that we've taken differing affections and tried to describe them with one limited English word. The framework of the word is just not that universally applicable. If we apply it in its biblical contexts of agape, storge, or philia, then we should denote the differences when speaking our languages of today. I believe eros in exclusive use should not be referenced in the same context as God's love. It's unfortunate how we have conditioned ourselves with language so as to speak negativity into something as beautiful as love. Many of us incorrectly reference the intended joy and pleasures of love and/or marriage with phrases like "falling in", "in the bonds of," or "within the confines of". Well, those don't sound like positive or voluntary "conditions" to me. Additionally, pleasures certainly apply more to a love union than a confinement. I believe if we change our perceptions, we probably also change our experiences. We'd all much rather ascend to something, than fall in anything.

The answer to the heading of this chapter speaks to the essence of true love! In Greek culture, the word agape did not have the powerful meaning used in biblical references. Agape love was given elevated context by New Testament authors to convey the incomprehensible depth and breadth of God's valuation of mankind. Because God's love is unconditional it does not exist as a function of reason. It never possesses a targeted attribute. In other words, in order to love like God, we would need to value a person holistically all the time.

Our initial targeted attraction is the reason we like something or someone, and in the process of cultivating a relationship we may (or may not) ascend to love . . . God, however, needs not like us to love us. I use the term ascend deliberately. However, the pinnacle of ascension experienced by most humans is philia. If we truly get there, we will have formed a common bond that cannot be broken. We will enjoy the pleasures within this connection for life. But, don't feel like your life is limited if you are unable to truly understand or convey God's love (agape) towards other human beings. There's a reason He's God, and we're human beings. God knows our limits. That's the reason Jesus came to be the living example of His love for us. When we understand and accept this Gift, we are then truly able to enjoy the love he intended for us to experience.

Real love (agape, storge, or philia), by the way, has no defined time-line. It could literally develop at first sight; or over a number of years. When the connection is made, the ties that bind us to the ones we love overcome any possible issues that might normally tear us apart. The only way we know we are in a love relationship is when the feeling of oneness is still pervasive at the other person's worst. The marriage between my parents has certainly experienced ascension in love. I've seen an intentional increase in oneness by their efforts. Even through the storms of life their love has never failed.

Now for the qualifying principle: I referenced both love and ascending in love. These separate "connections" may or may not exist concurrently. The first you can have without the second. We can love without being in love. That means the object of our love does not love us back. Being "in love" romantically though requires that proven reciprocal love exists between two individuals! The ability to reason is an absolute necessity for being in this form of intimate love! The proving of our love comes during the "ascension in". Once genuinely IN, our actions should not be indicative of proving it; but of expressing it. Remember to not psychologically debilitate ourselves by the words we use. Proof is necessary evidence in a case involving doubt. Whereas expressions are complementary actions that support that which is already believed to be true! Always express your love to the one you love. If proof is needed, there is no love.

The Five Love Languages:
1. Words of Affirmation
2. Quality Time
3. Receiving Gifts

4. Acts of Service
5. Physical Touch

When we evaluate eros or philia love there are specific attractions for different people. We each have our own romantic love language/languages that fulfill us in a love relationship. Included are words of affirmation, spending quality time, receiving gifts, acts of service, and physical touch. Gary Chapman has an excellent book entitled "The Five Love Languages" in which he does a great job of explaining each. I recommend everyone read this book in order to clearly understand and communicate the love language in your relationship. When we are in love there is a physical, a spiritual, and an emotional attraction between the two parties. We take time to discover and express the love language/languages of our mate, knowing they will reciprocate. It takes two selfless individuals to successfully be in and sustain an in love relationship! Conversely, there is no way we can be in love if our love language is not being expressed to us!

Though love is a simple word, its use should not be taken lightly. Because we're scripturally enlightened that God is Love, we should be cognizant of such at all times. We can do nothing to earn His love. Yet, He gives it freely to us anyway. More revealing is the fact that we can't do anything to lose His love either. We should therefore understand the immense value in us that He's demonstrating. So in the future before professing "LOVE" for anyone, we should weigh whether or not we have ascended to a place of internal value for her/him that can never wane. THAT is LOVE!

Chapter 12

A Message to Women

When you reach the stage of life where you're ready to settle down it's also time to make an honest self assessment. You need to feel complete as a woman, because it won't be any man's job to do that for you. Make sure also that you are ready to let a man into your world. You have dedicated a lot of time and effort into building your life without a mate. Are you ready to share what you've created and give up your autonomy? Men are well aware that women are making more money now than ever before. The "Independent Woman Movement" has sprouted financially successful women in many industries. There are millionaire corporate executives like Irene Rosenfelds (CEO of Kraft Foods, Inc.) and self-made billionaires like Oprah Winfrey. Regardless of where you are along the career continuum, you must decide how a relationship fits within your plans before beginning one.

Before you begin dating is also the decision time for what type of relationship you're ready to commit. Are you ready for only casual dating, a serious relationship, or maybe even marriage? Whichever it is, make sure to communicate it to your suitors. I purposefully don't offer advice on "casual dating" because I don't have a mature perspective to share. There are things that I did as a boy that I would never subject myself to as a man. I can't imagine doing anything casually that might possibly compromise pertinent elements of my well being—like my emotional and physical health. I was admittedly rusty with the differing modes of today's dating scene a couple of years ago after my marriage of 14 years ended. So I was in for a rude awakening. A woman who expressed a mutual interest actually shared with me that she was already "kind of seeing someone". Yet, she was interested in getting to know me. Well, I'm not one for tossing around hearts and seeing where they land—mine, hers, or the other guy's—so I politely declined advancing the relationship. The fact was that if she was already okay with "kind of seeing someone," then what would prevent her from "kind of seeing me?"

For any other couple, regardless of what the expectation may be, it's important that it's shared by each person. In the case of marriage a very important element of compatibility is each person's expectations regarding children. Honesty in relationship expectations should not be viewed lightly. Be up front and sincere with men about your desires; and believe him when he reveals his to you. Don't ever go into a relationship having differing objectives with the expectation that you can change him. This is a recipe for disaster.

Be cognizant of how you present yourself to potential mates. How your man treats you oftentimes is a direct reflection of the perceptions and expectations taken from the circumstances that drew you together. If this was classy, respectful, and honorable, the relationship is more often than not similarly nurtured. Sadly, relationships formed after less honorable meetings also tend to form with less honorable expectations. Sure, there are exceptions to these patterns. But, why risk it with possibly the most important type of interpersonal relationship you will experience. So don't expect to meet your prospective soul mate as the party animal at the club, yet be treated like a respectable lady at home. Unfortunately, life doesn't readily accept such contradictions of womanhood.

Preparing ourselves for serious dating is no different than getting ready for an important job interview. You must present yourself as the woman you want to be viewed as all the time. Contrary to the misguided belief and actions of some, real men prefer classy women over trashy facades every day of the week. The former are actually who we find most sexy. One or two bad decisions can change your positive image in an instant.

I believe ALL women deserve to be treated as our Queens. It doesn't matter to me whether you are a believer in Christ; or a Jew, Muslim, or Atheist. If you are a woman, you should be treated like a Queen. It has nothing to do with how you look; how you dress; how educated you are; or any other superficial measurement. But, because you are a human being created by God for a special purpose; regardless of what it may be. A very unique one is being the mothers of humanity. Your Queendom starts with you though. Be respectable, and the right man will show you respect. Be honorable, and he will honor you. Be loving, and he will love you back.

Ladies present who you are and the correct man will take notice. You only have control of you. So don't expect to find a man and change him into what you want. Be patient in preparing yourself to be the right woman, then you'll have a better grasp of who the right man is for you. Don't fall for the lie that there are no good men. Men's hearts are just as big as those of women, just as able to love, and just as subject to breaking. You must be mindful though of the fact that we are different.

There are common emotional needs amongst men, just as there are for women. If you care enough to discover and execute them, then you're more likely to find and keep the man for you. The following are high propensity areas that often lead to problems when neglected by women within relationships:

1. **Sexual fulfillment**—Don't neglect your man sexually. There are certain temptations that we face in life that are unnecessary. I will never excuse cheating, but I will tell you that a satisfied appetite doesn't hunger for more.

2. **Recreational companionship**—As your man's best friend, you are also the companion he would enjoy most. You should show an interest and participate in his leisure activities with him. You might find some of those 4-hour ventures on the golf course useful for having productive conversations with your man.

3. **Aesthetic appeal**—Men are visual creatures; and as crass as it may sound, we probably were not looking at your personalities when we first found you attractive. Maintaining your looks demonstrates to your man that you are just as sensitive to pleasing him today as you were in attracting him in the beginning. Yes, we are aware that women's bodies experience changes with pregnancy. Even so, you can make an effort to keep yourself attractive for your mate.

4. **Domestic support**—It is often joked that the way to a man's heart is through his stomach. There is actually some truth to this idiom. Family roles have changed over the years though. And with dual career households, men are sharing more of the domestic duties with women than ever before. Some view traditional roles in the home as chauvinistic. However, they are still valued by most men. They view the more physical chores (i.e. heavy lifting and yard work) as the responsibility of the husband, and the more domestic chores (i.e. cooking and caring for the children) as duties of the wife. Regardless of how the duties are decided, coming home to a peaceful and organized home is important to most men.

5. **Admiration**—there's no better feeling for a man than to know he's held in high regard by his woman. Be sure to encourage your man, and share how proud you are of him. When a man knows that he's admired at home, the challenges of the outside world are much easier to face.

Don't get so caught up in feminism, or the women's independence movement, that you view relationships as more antagonistic competitions than loving commitments. We are to be bonding, not contending. Furthermore, successful relationships—particularly marriages—are unions, not partnerships. There is no dividing line of who owns what. Both people own 100% of what should now no longer be viewed as mine and yours, but ours. Financially secure men are well aware that financially secure women don't need them in a material sense of provisions. So we need not continue hearing that. Fruitful relationships blossom only when the parties develop enough trust to become reciprocally vulnerable and dependent. The need expressed in these matured relationships is not materialistic. It's about a spiritual and emotional connection.

Although some immature males feel threatened by your success, a real man will not. I personally can appreciate my wife's ability to thrive independently before our union. This was definitely a positive characteristic. It assures me that she is with me because she wants to share a life with me, not because she needs to in order to meet the practical essentials of living.

It's time ladies to put aside any negative experiences you've had with boys and prepare for the love of a man. The guy who sat around your house lazily and pilfered off your hard work and resources with no attempts at contributing is not a man. The guy who impregnated you and ran as soon as you shared the news with him is not a man. The guy who sleeps with every woman he possibly can while claiming to love and care for you is not a man. And any guy who would dare raise his hand against a woman in anger is not a man. Real men behave like gentlemen and treat women like the precious people they are. They also understand what they want, and go after it. A true soul mate is a precious find for a real man. He will be eagerly loving, respectful, faithful, selfless, honest, forgiving, loyal, and trustworthy. You'll just need to reciprocate the same.

Chapter 13

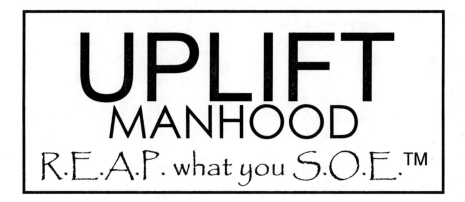

A Message to Men

Men, we spend a great deal of time in our love relationships trying to prove our manhood! I submit to you that this is wasted time. Likewise, we have mistakenly associated sensuality and intimacy with a loss of masculinity. Nothing could be farther from the truth. What better display of manhood is there in a relationship than to satisfy the physical and emotional desires of your lady? The flower that blossoms from this adoration will share with the world that you're "The Man".

What makes us unique individually and within a properly united relationship is the sovereignty of our own interpretations of love. In other words, if we ourselves define successful expressions of love within our relationships then we have the best chance for happiness. External opinions of what love is or is not would not affect us. The two people in the relationship need just be in sync. As men we need to asked our women what they like and if we love them it should be our pleasure to oblige.

As is the case with men though, there are also common emotional needs amongst women. The following are high propensity areas that often lead to problems when neglected by men within relationships:

1. **Affection**—Whereas men are more likely to be desirous of physical intimacy, women seek the intimacy of an emotional connection. This is evident in the way you speak to her, how you look at her, how you touch her, being chivalrous for her, and expressing other loving acts that show your more sensitive side. "It's the thought that counts" is a very important mantra for men to remember regarding the commemoration of meaningful dates for their women. Showing your woman that you care by sharing a token of your appreciation of her is important. Be proactive in celebrating important dates like birthdays and anniversaries. It's not so much what you purchase for these events, as much as having remembered them. A gift is another expression of your love for her. Additionally women are moved by "just because" gifts. These are important representations that show we care for them all the time, not just on special occasions.

2. **Open Communication**—Make talking with your woman a priority. She should never be made to feel that you're too busy for her. As our woman's best friend we should serve as the empathetic ear when she needs to talk. Women also desire that we share with them as well. Being able to communicate clearly and effectively with our women is an important key to a peaceful relationship. Women desire that men be open and honest with them. The sanctity of the relationship is very important. Anything that needs to be discussed and sorted out must be done so within the relationship before outside people are involved. If you have skeletons in your closet, your woman should not have the potential to be blind-sided with them from a third party.

3. **Financial Support**—It's important for women to feel like they have a provider at home. This does not necessarily mean that the man is bringing home the largest piece of the financial pie. However, it is important in most cases to women that he is a productive

financial contributor to the household. It is also important that you set the standard for the house by spending responsibly. Your example shows proper stewardship of your resources, in addition to being a training tool for your children on appropriate handling of finances.

4. **Family Commitment**—Women are fond of men executing the Head of Household role. In families with children, particularly pertinent is parenting support as an actively engaged father. You should jointly plan and participate in the raising of your children. Be active in setting, supporting, and implementing the house rules. Also, being noticeably present for important moments in the children's lives like the first day of school, doctor's appointments, and extra curricula activities shows her that family is a priority to you.

Regardless of the politically correct times in which we live, men and women are fundamentally different beings . . . A gentleman's chivalry should never cease; and a lady's domestic virtues should never wane! Those who continue to fight for sameness—instead of oneness—will just continue a trend of aloneness! Insecurity is unbecoming of real manhood (or womanhood). Don't feed it with inattentiveness to the needs of the woman you love.

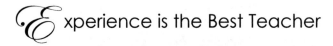

*E*xperience is the Best Teacher

Relationship experts and marriage counselors offer advice on what we should do to find love, make it blossom, or rekindle the fire within our current relationships. Many of these individuals have great information. However, I still measure their credibility in personal relativity in their own lives, not theory. I've recently read a number of criticisms of comedian Steve Harvey's books that offer advice to women about men. After Steve's ex-wife surfaced with claims of infidelity the social networks and blog sites became particularly busy. There were specific references to his discussion of the three things (The "3 P's" as Steve calls them) that a man will do if he truly loves you: "*profess his love for you publicly, protect you by any means necessary, and provide for you even if it means there is nothing left for himself."* I believe wholeheartedly in these traits of a man in love.

However, many critics seem to be unable to get past Steve's alleged dark past. A number of ladies from the "Independent Women" movement believe they don't need to be provided for or protected. It appears that these women discount Steve's views as chauvinistic. For critics, there are two points I'd like to make:

1. Steve's credibility appears to be called into question for something that even if true, is an element of his past. Some people seem to stop with the sin as if there were no redemption. If we do that with everything, then instead of sharing opinions 99% of people would need to remain 99% mute. A biblical perspective on any of Steve's possible past improprieties tells us that sin has no hierarchy. There's a passage in which Jesus challenged those who were to stone a woman found guilty of adultery: " . . . If any one of you is without sin, let him be the first to throw a stone at her." (John 8:7) Not a single stone was thrown. No one cast a stone because no one is without sin. With Steve, I personally see wisdom in the advice from a battle-tested survivor who lost some past battles but made it through the fight!

   Steve Harvey is a comedian, not a relationship guru. However, he is also a man. He is an extremely well-known public figure who appears to acknowledge his foibles. He certainly relates more to the masses than those "celebrities" whose publicists would have you believe that their behinds don't stink! God uses people from all backgrounds, and allows His light to shine through them!

2. My second point speaks to the accusation of chauvinism. Some ladies seem to inject duality into Steve's beliefs, as if these attributes of a man's love for his woman preclude the same attributes in themselves. That was never stated or implied by Steve from what I read. Although the expressions may be different, both the man and woman can reciprocate these elements of love. I profess my love for my wife from the mountaintop; I will protect her with my life; and I will provide for her with my last. I also know that she

will do the same for me. This is manifested both physically and emotionally, though sometimes differently.

As is relevant in many areas of our lives, personal experience provides us with great opportunity. We can learn grand lessons from our failures that serve us well into our futures. The key is to not continue to repeat the same mistakes over and over again. This is the essence of wisdom.

Opportunities also exist for us to learn from others. It's certainly not an absolute necessity that we repeat the blunders of those who've walked similar journeys before us. However, I've found the Principle of Personal Relativity relevant in deciding from whom I'm most likely to accept a credible lesson. As was the case with the safari guide and the lion attack, if I'm facing a problem in my relationship it's probably best that I speak with someone who has faced and overcome a similar problem, than someone who never has.

Having failed miserably a couple of times before I met the one in my own life, I have many transferable lessons as well. In keeping with my *Principle of Personal Relativity*, my directives are on the behaviors of men. In order for our relationships to thrive we must deliberately romance the passion into them. There should be playful touches throughout the day. Be sure to open doors for your woman. Buy flowers for her for no particular reason. Write her love notes/poems. Speak lovingly to her at all times . . . yes, all the mushy stuff! It amazes me how many men want "flowers", yet treat their wives or girlfriends like thorns! Success in a relationship just as in life is a choice. We can be productive or destructive. Our results will reflect these choices.

Chapter 14

$\mathcal{T}$he Mirage Principle™

Is your relationship steadfast or stumbling? Steadfast relationships are maintained through clear and consistent communication. Each of our perceptions are also our individual realities. So our assumptions may not necessarily coincide with our significant other's assumptions. Human nature is drawn to empathy and intimacy. Beware when we're not showing empathy, because someone else soon will be! This principle is applicable to any type of relationship. However, the potential stakes within romantic relationships (especially marriage) are usually higher.

I named this The Mirage Principle™. From a practical perspective, a dehydrating person needs (not just wants) water. The need can be so overwhelming when stranded in a desert that that people lose all sense of reason. They will visualize oasis containing what appears to be life-saving water. Unfortunately these are illusions they can't distinguish from reality because of their altered mental state. Before they realize what hit them, they fill themselves with sand, further threatening their chances of survival. The same is the case for neglected empathy and/or intimacy within our relationships. The neglected person is starving for an actual emotional need and will eventually have it filled one way or another. Far too often it's filled by a "mirage." The "mirage" may be someone who's taking advantage of his/her vulnerability. In other cases, the void is artificially filled in a manner that detracts from their emotional and/or physical health. We can selfishly complicate love if we so choose, but we can also choose to be attentive to the needs of our loved ones (in their love language) and enjoy the "fruits" of the way the union is intended.

The secret of loving is really no secret at all, but a willingness to apply the intrinsically selfish concern for our own happiness to another individual. They, in turn, reciprocate. There is no neglect in this scenario. In a proper union, when we love deeply, we will also be deeply loved! Submission, though not traditionally associated with a man's role within a love relationship, is a mutual necessity. It's not a release of our wills, but rather a willingness to release our hearts to the appropriate woman. When the pairing is right, the "head" and "body" of the union have equal consideration. They each proactively and consistently attend to the needs of the other! Many men communicate their own love language to the ones they love instead of communicating the love language of the ones they love! We can't speak a foreign language and expect to communicate clearly! Each woman's perception of our actions is her reality. Let's make sure we know what that is!

"The secret of loving is really no secret at all, but a willingness to apply the intrinsically selfish concern for our own happiness to another individual. They, in turn, reciprocate."

Chapter 15

$\mathcal{W}$hen is it time to move on?

Obviously, almost no one starts a relationship in expectation of it coming to an end. And certainly no one gets married to get divorced. Nevertheless, as a God fearing man I firmly believe that there are times we make our own relationship choices that are not His will for us. Therein we certainly learn life lessons as in any other experience. It's not God's nature to line up with mankind. To the contrary, until we align with His will, we can expect to reap the consequences of the mortal decisions we've sewn.

Many of my fellow believers use biblical references to validate their choices to remain in emotionally, spiritually, and even physically degrading marriages. The biblical dictum for lifelong unions shared by Jesus was *"Therefore what God has joined together, let man not separate."* (Matthew

19:6 & Mark 10:9) We human beings have taken this out of context to justify that any person we decide we'd like to marry is a God-ordained union. Well, not all of them are. By no means am I saying we should just walk out on marriages that don't seem to be working. Make a sincere effort to repair and rebuild the relationship first. If it doesn't work and the degradation continues, only then should we leave.

Before leaving, all the costs must be weighed, including how the decision will affect other people. There are usually huge ramifications to a divorce. Each of the parties will be affected financially, emotionally, and sometimes even physically. If children are involved, they will surely be affected as well, and should be considered. However, never let children be the only reason to stay in a marriage. It does our kids no favors having them observe an empty marriage of dissenting parents. The façade will set an extremely poor example of what marriage should look like for them one day. We marry our spouses, not our kids. So if a divorce is necessary, we should only divorce our spouses, not our kids. Far too often we make bad choices, and suffer the consequences accordingly—my first-hand experience in this area included. But my life experiences have never been just about me. I've had to endure the realities of divorce financially and emotionally. However, my children receive just as much love and support from both parents as they always have. Just because parents are not under the same roof, children don't have to feel emotionally divided. The adjustment the children have made to this unfortunate reality has been amazing. God has blessed me in many ways to be a resource and blessing to others, even in my setbacks.

"Loving our mate is a privilege; not a chore."

Togetherness

We will surely encounter challenges in this life. They should be faced together in relationships—not created by them. Loving our mate is a privilege, not a chore. I find our descriptions of relationships can be quite prophetic. We often refer to "working" on our relationships; rather than to cultivating a life together! For whatever reason we have been conditioned to believe that relationships must be a difficult undertaking. Even some experts tell us it's healthy to sometimes have quarrels within our relationships. I don't believe that either of these is truth. Correctly joined unions aren't difficult, and anger is never a successful catalyst to conflict resolution. Who really wins an argument anyway? Two relentless warriors will perpetually remain engaged in battle. This dissension carries with it reciprocal detriment, regardless of who's presumably "winning" the fight. Regardless, neither is able to enjoy the benefits of peace. So, the argument is won by he/she who ceases to argue!

Again, I am not recommending that we flee relationships at the first sign of trouble. Relationships will be challenging because two separate individuals form one union. There are tests to this coming together that should be expected as each party learns more about the other. Each sifts through commonalities and differences for compatibility. Before a commitment is made, though, the essentials of a productive relationship should have been revealed and vetted. Because we are fallible people, perfection is not our gauge for success. Still, the journey should never be viewed as work. When disagreements occur, they should not be exacerbated by arguments, but resolved by loving discussions. I observed a great example of this in my parents. They've had disagreements over the years, but they have found a way to resolve them with civility every time. They've never viewed marriage or any element of their relationship as a competition. It's a journey of challenges they face together. We would all be wise to do the same.

We are to keep our love simple, but deliberate. Because of all the negativity in the world today, we truly need sanctuary within our love relationships. We are to be considerate of each other; patient, kind, and comforting. We should speak and act lovingly towards our mates whom we love. In relationships where we embrace the acts of loving and being loved we will ascend and have peace! These are personal choices that should be viewed as privileges of the commitments we make—not obligations within them. Viewing them as obligations is a sure sign of trouble. There is a distinct difference between a commitment and an obligation: A commitment is a responsibility of internal choice, whereas an obligation is a responsibility of external assignment. I unfortunately found myself in marriage drifting away from this simple way of loving. Disagreements were not being handled civilly, and my role was definitely beginning to feel obligatory!

My personal decision to divorce didn't occur from some sudden occurrence. The caution signs that we are in a misaligned relationship usually have an evident reveal at some point. Unfortunately, we'll too often choose to ignore them, because the other person has some other attributes that are pleasing to us. We at times connect with a person whose personality we like, but when we get to know their true character, we find incompatibility. This does not necessarily mean that either person is bad; it just means they are incompatible—i.e. they are bad for each other.

Too often we fall into the trap of assimilating certain behaviors in order to impress someone we like. Facades can't last forever, though. So eventually the real character is revealed. Some areas of a person's character may not be evident to us when we are in the "honeymoon" stage of a relationship. We are both demonstrating our best—which can unfortunately mask our norm. Compatibility is best found in normal behaviors, not special presentations.

I believe that many things change in relationships for various reasons. However, changes in circumstances don't qualify as changes in one's character. A couple truly in love doesn't let kids, careers, or any other ancillary aspect of their relationship get in the way of their passion for each other. That's why we are to make sure we know our chosen one in all areas of compatibility—and before we commit to him or her. Love relationships are not a business arrangement—which is why they are called "love"! If we lack compatibility in any essential area of our connection, then we are setting ourselves up for a life of compromise. We are human beings and fallible in every sense of the word . . . so we're asking for trouble if we think we can build a solid and lasting love relationship around perpetual compromise!

There are 6.8 billion people on earth (300+ million in the U.S. alone). With those numbers, it would serve us all well to heed the signs of incompatibility and make a more informed decision before accepting any one of them. Obvious issues like infidelity and/or abuse are easy to associate with relationship failure. But not all "caution signs" are as conspicuous. The following are compatibility characteristics to discern:

1. The primary element of a person's character that reveals his/her misalignment is inconsistency. Principled people don't change whenever the wind blows. If you have someone who appears to be multiple people—someone with changed attitudes and behaviors to life's challenges—then you are receiving a sign. Is this a personality with which you can mesh?
2. Dishonestly is unacceptable. The first lie you are ever told is a tell-tale sign. Why allow someone to build a relationship on falsehoods? Keeping up with the intricacies of all the components of a lie is too much work. Eventually the truth will be revealed! Ultimately, what you see and experience (not necessarily what you hear) is what you will get in the end!
3. Disorganization of personal space is a cautionary sign. Unfortunately, sloppiness displayed externally is too often not just an external neatness problem. It can be reflective of turmoil

within. Even in exceptions, the presence of external disorder speaks to a decision that they are willing to dwell in chaos. Are you? An affirmative answer obviously exacerbates the chaos. Of course there are also exceptions that occur conversely—as in the case of individuals with Obsessive Compulsive Disorder (OCD). In these instances the internal anxiety may be expressed through an external obsession like excessive organization. These will certainly fall in the minority though. We have to make an honest evaluation of our lives and decide if peaceful surroundings are of value to us . . . and if so, this sign is a significant deterrent to a good relationship. If order is important to you, make sure you discuss that before committing yourself to someone who appears to not have a high regard for it!

4. Irresponsible handling of finances is to be avoided. This is not the same as falling on hard times due to job loss or our current economic recession. Rather, it is someone perpetrating a fraudulent lifestyle. The fraud is in whether they can afford their way of life via outright purchase, or are they living on credit? Additionally, do they pay their recurring bills on time? Joining with someone who's perpetually in debt and/or mismanaging finances will likely put you there eventually as well. As the saying goes "I can do bad all by myself"—we don't need help with that! If you are doing well, why invite someone who compromises that at the onset of the relationship? S/he need not be on your same economic level, but shouldn't be a threat to yours either. Their past habitual handling of finances is likely to be a precursor of their future behavior in this area as well.

5. Incompetence is a bad sign. If you have someone who can hardly ever do anything right and is constantly making excuses for failure, you have a flashing red light. We are gifted differently. So we should not expect everyone to be competent at everything. However, that to which we commit, we should competently complete. Otherwise we're displaying incompetence in either the promise or the execution. Either way, repeated returns of incomplete results are products of excuses, not reasons. Plainly put, "excuses are tools of incompetence used to build monuments of nothingness; and those who use those tools of incompetence

become monuments of nothingness!" Nothingness is certainly not conducive to productive relationships.

6. Broken promises are unacceptable regardless of how small the promise. We all have choices in life and as adults we have a choice to commit or not. If we commit to something/someone and don't follow through we are proving ourselves untrustworthy. Heed the tell-tale sign given you early in the small things, because big things will have bigger consequences. Promises are only as valid as the trustworthiness of the people executing them.

7. Discovering that the person with whom we're in a relationship is commitment-phobic is a sure sign of trouble. We must discuss and agree to the parameters of the relationship in the beginning. If it's defined as casual by one person, then it must be for both. Likewise, if our objective is a serious long term relationship then so must be the other person's. We all undergo various changes in our lives as we grow and mature. However, we should never base a relationship objective around a need for change in the individual with whom we're in the relationship. We must actually love who we are with today, not who we think they may become tomorrow. If we discover our relationship objectives are not congruent with our mate, then we must make the decision to protect our hearts from impending danger. A sure way to have our hearts broken is to commit ourselves to an individual who's not ready for a commitment.

8. Observing our mates interaction within longstanding relationships is supremely important to our decision to form a serious relationship with them ourselves. Familial relationships are the most natural human bonding we will all experience in life. People of the same lineage have an intrinsic relativity and perspective that can rarely be duplicated. We each act most natural when they're around. Additionally, longtime friendships share a unique bond that reveals a lot about us. In sum, our true character will be prominently on display within these interactions. These are people that know each of us well, and we will more than likely be the best representation of ourselves in their presence. It's important to meet these people, and examine the interactions between them and your mate. If you observe unacceptable behaviors or other cautionary signs, then these are likely to eventually display in

his/her interactions with you as well. Then would be the time to discuss this with them—and decide if these are behaviors with which you can live.

We often hear people blame failed relationships on something that occurred "all of a sudden", or by sharing "it just happened." Nothing happens "all of a sudden" and "it didn't just happen!" Our lives are divinely designed, and we are given the option of "quit" way before "stop" happens. The Principle of Personal Relativity works, so we can learn our lessons by heeding wise counsel; or by the often not-so-delicate lessons of experience. The choice is ours!

Chapter 16

The Best Relationship Confidant(e)

As a lifestyle coach and motivational speaker I've had many opportunities to dialogue with others on dating, marriage, or just general relationship etiquette. What I've found interesting is the relative consistency of choice for "adviser" friends by most men and women. As might be expected, men most often choose other men, as "relationship confidants", and women likewise choose other women. We are certainly creatures of habit. Unfortunately though, habits perpetuate in both good and bad choices. In our relationships, it would behoove us all to break habits that aren't accomplishing the intended results.

How do most of us answer the question "who is our confidant(e)?" We tend to choose a confidant(e) to whom we can relate—often, a confidant(e) of the same gender. Relativity is certainly an important trait for a trusted adviser (reference The Principle of Personal Relativity). However, what most of us miss is that the relationship confidant(e) should relate to our significant other! The analyst I am today wonders why I ever thought my male friends served as the best relationship confidants regarding the complexities of women. Why did I think they understood the underlying meaning behind certain female behaviors, and how best to respond lovingly? This is not something I've realized quickly or easily. It took about twenty years for my "light bulb" to switch on.

I'll skip the chase and get to the point. Over the years, I have received the most useful, relevant, and truthful advice on women from women. Unfortunately for me, I needed a few hard falls in relationships to accept the wisdom that 20/20 hindsight provides.

My first opportunity to learn from women about women would have probably saved me the biggest heartache I experienced as a young man: the failure of my relationship with my college sweetheart. This was my first love. Prior to college I was so focused on pursuing other life objectives that I didn't even consider having a serious girlfriend. Initially, I continued the same strategy at college. My first year was strictly about school and football. Any social activities were fun only—nothing serious.

Well, that changed my second year when I met who I felt was the love of my life. We had the proverbial whirlwind romance, with many of the usual (and some maybe not-so-usual) ups and downs. Prior to the start of this relationship, I had already established a few really strong male and female friendships at college. By the time I met my college girlfriend during my sophomore year, my friends had a pretty decent grasp on who I was.

I would share my normal relationship concerns with both my male and female friends. The guys seemed to always have a similar perspective to mine, whereas the ladies would have information that made me think. One of my female friends who spent a considerable amount of time with my girlfriend and I shared things with me that rang loudest and most relevant. She never had a negative thing to say about my girlfriend. She would primarily tell me what I needed to be doing to be pleasing to her, based on the type of person she observed my girlfriend to be. The suggestions she made were not difficult to do, and I was not unwilling to do them. However, my error was in listening to my boys—who, like me, felt I didn't *need* to change. This was my first experience with the common relationship mistake of sincere love misdirected. In other words, when I didn't consistently express the love language of the one I loved, she didn't feel loved. My female friend saw something I didn't. Her last bit of advice to me was that my girlfriend would break my heart if the relationship continued as it was . . . unfortunately for me, she was right!

"This was my first experience with the common relationship mistake of sincere love misdirected. In other words, when I didn't consistently express the love language of the one I loved, she didn't feel loved."

Though painful at the time, this experience began a period of growth. It took a couple more huge failures to see as clearly as I do today. Today, I thank God for the experiences. Without them I would not have the blessings of wisdom and understanding. Now, I am open to receiving instruction from the fairer sex (and particularly so in relationships). That is not to say that the same-sex friendships have lost their value. I believe we should all establish "confidant(e)-level" relationships with both sexes. However, what I learned is that my number one "relationship confidante" to provide useful, relevant, and truthful advice on a relationship with my woman is a woman! And a particularly great source of wisdom is open dialogue between me and the woman to whom I'm committed.

Communication within the relationship is the key. My mom put it best in her comment about the strength of her and my father's marriage: "Make sure she is your best friend," she said. Additionally she shared "No third party should know anything about your relationship that you don't both know first!" Men, ask your woman how to love her. Women, ask your man how to love him! I'm blessed to know that my best relationship confidante is at home. So like never before, I now get to express and enjoy amazing love! Ladies and Gentlemen, you too can experience the same.

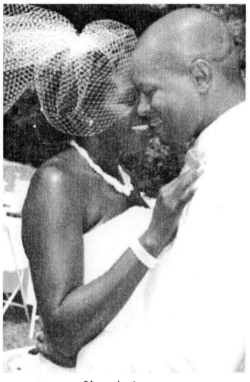

Simply Love

Chapter 17

UPLIFT
COMPANIONSHIP
R.E.A.P. what you S.O.E.™

"Most of us are well aware of the fact that we may have to kiss a few frogs before finding our prince or princess."

The Dating Game

It's amazing how natural dating is for us when we are in pursuit of a mate. We seem to be our most enthusiastic and creative during this time. Putting our best foot forward is the name of the game. This is true for both men and women. We demonstrate our most impressive self to someone who we may or may not like in the end. This is all a part of the discovery process. So as singles, many of us become aficionados of this dating game. Candlelight wining and dining is expected, and delivered often. We find ourselves replicating our best, time and time again, until we meet Mr. or Mrs. Right. Most of us are well aware of the fact that we may have to kiss a few frogs before finding our prince or princess.

When Mr. or Mrs. Right is finally found we seem to become drained of these once intrinsic desires to date. Instead of continuing to do things to impress our mates, we become complacent. In marriages this is exacerbated even more by the pressures of everyday family life. Career demands, finances, kids, and the monotony of daily routines take away from the time and energy that were once devoted exclusively to our mates. Unfortunately, this becomes the new norm for once vibrant love lives.

"Dating should be intentionally made a permanent fixture in all loving relationships. Stagnant complacency has no place in love."

We have a choice to not let our relationships descend to such a state of doldrums. Dating should be intentionally made a permanent fixture in all loving relationships. Stagnant complacency has no place in love. It's ridiculous to think that we would give so much effort in quest of our one true love. Then neglect him or her once the search is successful. We should be even more excited to date the person who we know is the ONE, as opposed to a prospect. The key to insuring this stays at the forefront of our plans is to actually include it in our plans. In other words, schedule date nights just as you do any other pertinent activity in your life. If your PATS order revealed Family & Friends near or at the top of your list, then there's no more important family member or friend than the one person to whom you've committed your life. Be sure to live your creed. The three little words are nice, but "I love you" expressed in actions speaks much more clearly.

"Think of each date as an opportunity to impress the love of your life."

Be creative and keep it fresh. I reference this part of our love life as "The Dating Game" because it should be a fun element we make high priority in our relationship. It shouldn't be viewed as an obligation of our commitment, but a privilege. Mix in places you like to visit often, along with new experiences as well. Think of each date as an opportunity to impress the love of your life. Do all the loving things you did when you first met: hold hands, whisper in each other's ears, open doors, and use mushy nicknames. These are all expressions that not only show your significant other that you care, but also remind you of the importance of the most impactful interpersonal relationship you'll experience in your lifetime.

Chapter 18

*W*ho's THE ONE?

So have you met the one? You know who I'm talking about: the one who knows what to say, and how to say it at exactly the right time; the one whose touch makes you feel like you've never felt before; the one who makes your eyes light up when he/she walks into a room; the one who looks at you like you have never been seen before; the one who honors you above all others. If you have found the one, don't ever let him/her go! I was asked by one of my friends if such a relationship existed, and if so could it last. Yes, it does exist and it does last! I've observed one for 40 of its 43 years. However, there are some traditional aspects that both men and women have to accept in order for modern-day relationships to have the same success. We must be willing to submit our lives to someone else.

Understand that submission within a relationship is not a sign of inferiority, but rather an expression of love. In a love relationship (particularly marriage) it is an absolute necessity. Both men and women must understand that submission is not a release of our wills, but a willingness to release our hearts to someone else. Too often, we have not had the patience to vet our suitors for proven qualities worthy of our hearts, so we are tempted to hold a little something back. Even if only one of the two in the union is being reserved, it will eventually cause problems. However, when the pairing is made correctly, both parties have equal consideration. They both consider it an honor to consistently and proactively attend to the needs and be there for each other. Thereby the two are one! The right love relationship has within it love expressions that keep you united even when you're physically apart . . . So, if you feel alone when you're with someone, then you're probably in the wrong relationship! It would be hard to see how that person could possibly be the *ONE*. I'm an absolute sponge of my parents' relationship now. I'm asking more questions and understanding more of the foundation underneath their action and inaction.

Understand that in order for our relationships to thrive we must form a union, not a partnership. The two must become one holistically. There are no longer *his* and *her* references. Everything is now ours. This is why trust is so important. We have literally given our lives to another person. Our romantic/marital relationships are in many cases the most life-impacting decisions we ever make . . . The wrong ones can be catastrophically debilitating; and the right one perpetually empowering!

"Understand that in order for our relationships to thrive we must form a union, not a partnership. The two must become one holistically. There are no longer his and her references. Everything is now ours."

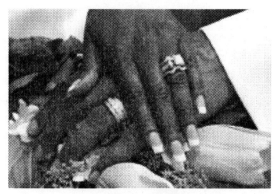

United as ONE

Chapter 19

he Honor of Parenthood

Becoming a parent is the most rewarding, yet challenging, role most people will ever experience. Parenting should be an adults-only undertaking. According to a 2009 report from the Centers for Disease Control and Prevention nearly 410,000 teen girls gave birth, which is 9 times higher than in other developed countries. This comes at an estimated cost of $9 billion to U.S. taxpayers. And the children from these environments start life with more of an uphill climb. Parenting should be for those people who are able and willing—financially, physically, and emotionally—to be held responsible and accountable for the development of other human beings. Effectiveness is measured by the degree to which their children mature to also display responsibility and accountability. The most successful parents are those who view this as an honorable privilege, and not a burdensome obligation.

This is the primary opportunity adults have to display their wares in The Principle of Nurturing. How well we do at training a child in the way they should productively live will be on full display in their relative production. In some rare cases, external influences may lead a child astray even with solid parenting at home. And then there are those who overcome negative home lives to be extremely productive. These are both of course exceptions, and not the norm of nurturing. Regardless, it's important to be a living testimony of our values.

Oftentimes kids seek external role models if they are unable to relate to a viable one close to or at home. The Principle of Personal Relativity should be on full display within every flourishing family. As parents, part of our role as mentors for our children involves showing them a positive way of living to which they might hope to aspire. This is found within values that can't be physically touched, but that do touch people's hearts.

Too often we hear children point to a well known celebrity—oftentimes an athlete or entertainer—as someone they most admire. This is an unfortunate trend of our society today. We don't have to be famous or wealthy in order to serve as positive role models for our children. Those are only superficial attributes of perceived success. Also, our children won't be limited by our accomplishments for actually admiring us. However, having tangible inspirations under the same roof provides clearer direction during formidable years than "role-models" in need of interpretation from a distance. It's likely that many of the well publicized rich and famous people of the world are not who our children perceive them to be anyway. Influence is best demonstrated up close and in person. This requires presence, not presents.

It was very important to have both my parents present throughout my football career. There was an increased awareness around the degree to which my mom's enthusiasm grew for the sport. She became my biggest fan. Interestingly, I remember that my mom was initially not very fond of football. She didn't quite understand the brutality, and why exactly someone would actually want to crash into other human beings with all his might. Well, she married a man with a passion for it, and had two sons who shared the same passion. She therefore intentionally developed an interest as her husband's favorite leisure time companion, and as a supportive mother.

During many of my presentations I share an experience drawn from the 1979 football season of my Pee Wee team of nine and ten year olds. I was nine years old at the time, and a rather talented running back. My team and I had gained many accolades that season. We were undefeated at 12—0, including two play-off wins. I earned the nickname "Slick-Man Tim" gaining over 1500 yards, while scoring 36 rushing touchdowns on the season. But, there was one more game to be played. It was the *Super Bowl* Championship Game against another excellent team whose only loss on the season was against us. The top player on the team was a friend of mine, Ooyiman Crumbly (now Ooyiman Muhammad). After a hard fought game of two very evenly matched teams it came down to a "made for the movies" moment. The game was tied 6—6, and no one was able to give us a clear explanation of what would happen in case of a tie (i.e. were there overtime rules, or would we just have co-champions). Our objective was to not have it come to that. It was a 4th and Goal play with our offense on the 3 yard line and 4 seconds on the clock. As we gathered in the huddle with family members and friends crowding the sidelines near the endzone I could almost hear my heart beating in anticipation of what was to come. I could also see my mom and dad among the parents. The intensity on my mom's face was energizing, even from a distance. I don't think there was anyone present unaware of who would be getting the ball on the final play. Our quarterback Morris Thomas, affectionately known as *Knockie*, called the play—"Strong Right Pitch Left, Ready . . . BREAK." Then he looked me in the eyes and said "Let's go Tim!" The play appeared to unfold in slow motion. Knockie went through his normal cadence, "Down, Set, Hut!" He pivoted out to his right and pitched the ball to me going left. Ooyiman's coach had him mirror me all day on their defense. He had done a great job of shutting me down up to that point. But this was for all the marbles. I could actually see him when I got the pitch. He appeared like a fire breathing dragon with steam coming from his breath in the cold air of that November night. It was *Showtime*. I began running around the left side towards the pylon and got a boost of energy I never expected. As I looked to my left I could see my mom appearing to jump like a jack rabbit above the crowd higher than anyone else. Although I couldn't hear a thing, I could see the forming of the words from her lips,

"GO TIM!" The next thing I knew I had outrun everyone to the corner of the endzone. By the time Ooyiman got to me it was too late. In frustration, he tackled me anyway. But he was my boy . . . I understood. With the time on the scoreboard now down to all zeros and the score reading 12—6, my mom raised me in her arms and kissed me as the rest of the parents, along with my teammates and coaches celebrated the triumph. Sharing that intense, yet brief experience with my mom was the best sports moment of my entire football career.

"Being proud of my parents drives me to make sure I remain someone of whom they can be proud as well."

As I shared before, my parents have never attained the financial success I did early in my adulthood. But looking up to their examples served as powerful inspiration to get me there. Being proud of my parents drives me to make sure I remain someone of whom they can be proud as well. Their admirable traits have nothing to do with superficial or material things. Sharing the core principles of their faith in God with me so that I could make my own personal decision was imperative to my spiritual growth. Showing me that they care by actually being present in my life has been vital. Demonstrating a loving relationship between each other instilled that ideal within me for my own relationships. Observing great work ethic in them inspired the cultivation of one in me. Being people of integrity in their daily interactions also instilled that in me. And building quality relationships around me allowed me to see value in them through the expressions of others as well. This has allowed me to replicate the same for my children and share other life-skills I've acquired along the way. In my parents I've been able to see the clear execution of value-based drive with admirable contentment, as opposed to insatiable pursuits or unfulfilling complacency. They demonstrate joy and peace living within the lifestyle afforded them knowing that they've exhausted their best efforts. Insatiable pursuits are evident in people constantly in the rat race, who never get to experience peace in their lives. Complacency on the other hand settles for whatever results occur from marginal efforts that usually stop at the first sign of challenge. Mature parenting knows it's important to get this message communicated right. I thank God he gave me the Dynamic Two to instill His Principle of Nurturing in me.

"There is a definite financial responsibility to fatherhood; but by no means is it the primary one."

Mothers have traditionally been the most present parent during the formidable years for children. So developing the aforementioned admiration and respect from experiential observations oftentimes happens more consistently with them. Many of the physical activities in preparation for my football career took place with my father by my side. However, I remember having such a connection to my mother as a child that I felt if I lost her during my youth that I would not have survived. God obviously saw fit for me to not face such a challenge, as she continues to be a very present fixture in my life today. Thankfully though, she and my father did nurture me to maturity beyond such dependence.

Oftentimes, fathers must do more to make the same impact. And as a man my most relative wisdom on parenting is to other men. After a long talk with my dad one day I began to reflect on what his practical example and daily involvement really meant to me and my siblings during our youth. Particularly evident for me personally was the "How to's" of being a highly productive and responsible law—abiding citizen; while at the same time taking care of home. I've observed a number of single mothers—both voluntary & involuntary—raising children with no involvement from the man who contributed to their conception. No, these men do not get the title of "Father". That would be a disrespectful association for the men who do step up to the plate as they should. In no way do I want to belittle the efforts of the women, or the positive roles they play in the lives of their children. However, fatherhood plays a significant role in the development of children as well, but is often viewed as secondary. Far too many men are unaware of the void left behind when they fail to step up to this vital responsibility. There is a definite financial responsibility to fatherhood; but by no means is it the primary one. The best way for a boy to learn how to become a man is from first hand lessons from a man. And daughters will certainly understand what a quality man is like when they've been raised by one. I uncovered some research on the impact this noble role really plays in our society. The statistics below spoke loudly and clearly to me that our presence in the lives of our children is exponentially more valuable than our presents:

- **63%** of youth suicides are from fatherless homes. (Source: U.S. D.H.K.S., Bureau of the Census)
- **90%** of all homeless and runaway children are from fatherless homes. (Source: U.S. D.H.K.S., Bureau of the Census)
- **85%** of all children that exhibit behavioral disorders come from fatherless homes. (Source: Center for Disease Control)
- **85%** of all youths sitting in prisons grew up in a fatherless home. (Fulton County Georgia Jail Populations and Texas Dept. of Corrections, 1992)
- **80%** of rapist motivated by displaced anger come from fatherless homes. (Source: Criminal Justice & Behavior, Vol 14, p-403-26,)
- **71%** of all high school dropouts come from fatherless homes. (Source: National Principals Association Report on the State of High Schools)
- **75%** of all adolescent patients in chemical abuse centers come from fatherless homes. (Source: Rainbows for all Gods children)
- **70%** of juveniles in state-operated institutions come from fatherless homes. (Source: U.S. Dept. of justice, special report, Sept. 1988)

These facts translate to mean that children from a fatherless home are:

- **5 times more likely to commit suicide.**
- **32 times more likely to run away.**
- **20 times more likely to have behavioral disorders.**
- **14 times more likely to commit rape.**
- **9 times more likely to drop out of high school.**
- **10 times more likely to abuse chemical substances.**
- **9 times more likely to end up in a state-operated institution.**
- **20 times more likely to end up in prison.**

As men we should think about the impact of our decisions both positively and negatively. We have many lives depending on us. I often share with audiences that the first time I truly understood what unconditional love meant was when I became a father. As the father or mother of a child, we are vital elements in creating another person. Even science has proven that life starts at conception. No matter what happens after the pregnancy is confirmed, this new creation is a part of us, literally. My children are the only people in my life that I can say the relationships began, and will always exist without conditions. Of course my wife and I cultivated our relationship to develop unconditional love. However, as with any romantic relationship there was a point in time when we didn't even know each other. Therefore, there were elements of attraction that made us connect in the beginning. No matter how small or great a degree these existed, they were the conditions that grew the love. For a willing parent there are no conditions establishing a relationship with our children. They can be aesthetically attractive or disfigured, healthy or ill, smart or remedial, rich or poor. It matters not, they are still our children. We'll be given our greatest thrills through their achievements, and our deepest frustrations in their struggles. Regardless, those of us who're able to remain sane love them coming into the world, and do upon our exits out as well.

Even with this unique intrinsic connection to our children, the key to a successful marriage and productive parenting is understanding where children fit within the family structure. Ecclesiastes 4:12 shares the following: *"Though one may be overpowered, two can defend themselves. A cord of three strands is not quickly broken."* This verse is referenced often relative to the proper headship of families. In other words the family should be built around a foundation of Christ at the center of the relationship of the husband and wife. If a couple chooses to have children, then they should come underneath and compliment the marital union. As noble a role as parenting may be, it is not to be placed ahead of the marriage covenant between the husband and wife. Part of the decision process before having children should address how the marriage relationship will be maintained while growing a family. It will require a concerted effort and sacrifice. But it must be well thought out and planned. Career adjustments must be discussed; disciplinary methods should be decided; and budgetary modifications must be considered. But *The Dating Game* must continue. The relationship between husband and wife is the priority within successful families.

We actually schedule the children within our family's Dating Game. Besides our husband and wife dates, we also have family dates with everyone, and dates where we independently take the kids out to share one-on-one time. This allows them to each share conversation with us without competing for time with their siblings. It also gives us the opportunity to nurture proper dating etiquette within them. They have become well aware of how they should treat their future mates, and how they should be treated.

Kids are very adaptable and cunning. They will take as much rope as we give them. It's our responsibility though to not allow them to hang themselves. So it's best as parents to establish clearly defined house-rules early. And reiterate them often. I've shared a copy of what we use in our family at the end of this chapter. We all sign an agreement called "The Watson Family Covenant". There is no cookie cutter parenting handbook that will work for all families. However, the mother and father should agree on the family rules and structure. Keep in mind though that under Christ the husband is first subject to the wife, and the wife to the husband. The kids fall in line under this relationship.

"If the couple chooses to have children, then they should come underneath and compliment the marital union."

The Watson Family

WATSON FAMILY COVENANT:

Each member in this FAMILY will be treated with RESPECT. We all Love one another and our WORDS and ACTIONS should show it ALL THE TIME.

Our Parental Promise:

We promise to express LOVE to each of you daily with both PRAISE for your accomplishments; and CORRECTION when you err or misbehave. We will make sure to speak to you in a respectful tone and encourage you. We will treat each other with respect as well to demonstrate the tenderness and LOVE we expect each of you to exhibit towards us and one another. We will ALWAYS be OPEN to TALK with each of you about any problem you may have; no matter how BIG or SMALL. This is our promise to **Tre', Lexi, Christian, and our children to come**. Our "Praise Board" will be maintained for logging your accomplishments ("checks") and misbehavior ("X's) to make sure we all hold one another accountable for this Promise.

Rewards & Discipline will be noted as follows:

You each begin with an allowance amount weekly equal to your age... You will receive $.25 additional allowance for each "check" that you receive on your "Praise Board". Each week that you do not receive two or more X's you will receive $1 additional allowance. If you don't receive any X's during a given week you will receive $5 additional allowance. A reward "check" will be given as I see fit for exceptional DEEDS and/or BEHAVIOR.

Punishable Offenses:

1. Disrespectful behavior
2. Willful Disobedience
3. Inappropriate Language
4. Fighting with siblings
5. Lying

Punishment:

1. Each time one of the above offences is committed you will receive an "X" on your "Praise Board" & be grounded for a day (no TV, no playing games of any kind, no playing outside). In extraordinary cases of misbehavior you will receive a spanking of no more than five licks to the palm of your hand; or your behind.
2. If you receive three strikes within one week (Monday-Sunday), you will lose your allowance and be grounded for a week.

_____   _____
Parent's Signature   Date

_____   _____
Child / Children's Signature(s)   Date

SECTION V:

SYSTEMS OF EXCELLENCE

Chapter 20

$\mathcal{D}$iscovering our P.A.T.S.

Our decisions are primarily based on our needs. Practical needs include food, shelter, clothing, and transportation. Most will agree that these are essential for human beings to survive. Rationality would dictate that we make life decisions to insure their acquisition. However, human emotions carry much more weight in the choices we make than rationality. It's unlikely that any human being will make a significant choice without pulling something from within his/her core beliefs. This makes sound principles and character vital to choosing well.

What inspires us to do whatever we do will always drive us through the obstacles to getting it done. We must clearly identify our *inspirations* in order to achieve our *aspirations*. This is the motto of my coaching and motivational speaking practice. We as human beings are innately guided more by our inspirational/emotional drivers than we are the practical ones. So, the "why we do" is more meaningful to us than the "what we do." Unfortunately, many of us have never taken the time to clearly define and prioritize those drivers. So we may end up with different degrees of success, but not necessarily that which would equate to our personal sense of it. If we have truly identified our motivations and what success looks like to us, then we are more apt to persevere through life's challenges to reaching it.

"We must clearly identify our inspirations in order to achieve our aspirations."

Be sure to set quantifiable objectives. This is in contrast to the subjective and ambiguous setting of goals. In order to identify achievement, the achievement itself must be quantifiable, i.e., "I plan to meet with five coaching clients today" instead of "I'm planning to have an awesome day coaching." The first is a quantifiable objective, while the second is a subjective goal. My definition of awesome may not be the same as yours, so we have not effectively communicated if I can't quantify what will make the day awesome for me. Likewise, we shouldn't establish a plan that is so subjective that whether or not we have achieved it is dependent on someone's opinion, rather than on observable fact.

The one personal opinion that does weigh heavily in our success is our own opinion of what motivates/inspires us to action. I've termed this our "Proactive Attributions to Success" (PATS). The acronym PATS has dual meaning in this case because our own self-esteem (pats on the back) makes much more impact than the varying opinions of others.

Our PATS are those inspirational triggers that we can identify as reasons we do what we do. They are categorized in a manner that allows us to discover our own order of their place in our lives. The categories are all encompassing. No matter how trivial or important the activity; I promise you that we all can connect our reasons for doing it to one or more of the PATS listed below:

- **Faith**: Our moral code and/or spiritual belief system that guides us to do what we feel is right.
- **Family and Friends**: Important people in our lives with whom we value spending time.

- **Fortune**: All of our material possessions and/or money.
- **Fun**: Our leisure activities and/or hobbies.
- **Fame**: Our recognized achievements and/or status.

Throughout our lives we make most of our choices based upon these inspirational or emotional drivers. Just as the ACCT Profile is used to discern relationship influences and compatibility, our PATS uncover the motivation behind our actions. Here are two essential questions: (1) How well do we know our drivers? and (2) How conscientious are we about staying true to ourselves when we do?

To help you answer these questions, I formulated some tangible aids for PATS discovery, prioritization, and accountability. The first resource I created is UPLIFT values cards. These come in sets of five laminated cards; each has one of the PATS values on one side; and a brief definition on the back. I use these for PATS values discovery exercises during coaching sessions, as well as in my personal relationships. I also carry a set around in my pocket daily (in my prioritized order of course), as do many of my clients. The portability of the cards allows for fluidity of our list in case life changes necessitate a change in priorities. However, they still serve to make us conscious of what inspires us to continue on despite the obstacles. The second resource is something you create yourself: the PATS board. The PATS board has been extremely useful for me and my personal clients.

You can be as creative as you would like to be in building your personal "accountability partner". The materials I used for my personal board are a framed cork board (18 X 24), UPLIFT value cards, wallet-sized pictures, and tape. I placed the words of my prioritized list in order vertically on the board with enough space to insert my photographs of what each means to me. I used a cork board because my prioritized list may change as my life circumstances change, and I must be able to make adjustments if needed.

I truly believe in planning for success. We won't stumble upon it, and it doesn't occur by accident. We need tangible road maps to follow towards our clearly quantifiable objectives. However, these plans will never get fully realized without a heartfelt commitment.

Our prioritized PATS will provide the needed tug on our heartstrings. The order in which I have the PATS listed is my personal prioritized list. The list is just that though, my list. It will guide my path towards reaching my objectives successfully. Each of you must do the same thing in order to truly actualize your full potential and become all you were called to be. What you do will always have different meanings to different people. But why you do it can never be diminished by outside influence.

"We should cultivate our crafts, while carefully discerning outside pursuits."

Success does not have a universal appearance. Contrary to popular opinion it is a relative achievement. Engaging in persistent pursuits without the intended results is insane. We should cultivate our crafts, while carefully discerning of outside pursuits. This phrase is one of the basic considerations in order to develop the paradigm shift to extraordinary behaviors. Think of phrases commonly used to reference attaining success. We hear things like "seeking success," "chasing our dreams," and "in pursuit of excellence." All of these actions suggest that the intended end result cannot be engineered by utilizing our own internal talents (cultivated through our crafts). In each case success must be found or captured from some external source (a pursuit). A craft is primarily under our control. It is a creation utilizing our individual time and talents. A pursuit however is primarily out of our control. It is an external achievement, recognition, or position in which acknowledged advancement is subject to the opinion of others.

This book is a complete shift from that old way of thinking. I'm suggesting that we spend the majority of our time developing those things over which we have control, and limiting our pursuit of those things in which we do not. My suggested incorporation borrows from the Pareto Principle, also known as the 80/20 rule. Vilfredo Pareto was an Italian economist who discovered in the early 1900's that 20% of the population of Italy owned 80% of the land. Over the years others found the principle transferred into many other uses as well: including work production between employees, distribution of global wealth, and sales activity amongst clients of businesses. For purposes of the shift in our thinking needed to get the most from the principles shared within this book, my suggestion is that we spend 80% of our efforts on cultivating our crafts, and if we find it necessary to pursue distant dreams limit it to 20%. We are all purposefully gifted with specific talents for a specific purpose. So if we align our talents and purpose with our activities (professionally and personally), then success results. We author this free will decision. How true are you to you about you? If you wrote a book of your entire life's story, could you honestly categorize it as NON-FICTION? We must clearly identify our Inspirations in order to achieve our Aspirations.

My PATS Board

Chapter 21

The Success Pyramid

You have probably heard the phrase "climbing the ladder of success." This is a commonly used adage that I believe limits us to mediocre views of potential paths to success. When we take an honest look at the makeup of a ladder, I don't think we would really want to depend on such a flimsy vertical structure. With our lives on its rungs the stakes are particularly high. Yet ladders are extremely unstable. Laws of physics inform us that the higher we climb the more unstable they become. If we don't have them well secured, they're likely to topple over as we climb. Each of them has only one way up, and one way down. At the top there's room for but one person. So at some point during the climb we will each be impeded by the person above us regardless of our ability or motivation to continue. This is particularly frustrating if/when our abilities and motivation to climb supersede that of those already higher on the ladder. Our companions on life's journeys and the paths we choose are therefore vital to our success. Positive associations with other people and clearly defined paths are certainly important. But we should never align ourselves with people who impede our progress, or paths that limit our journeys. Unfortunately these pitfalls are inherent to a ladder, making it an unworthy "ascending tool" for planned excellence.

When looking for a more sound structure to cultivating a successful life my first consideration was stability. The basis of stability for anything is its foundation. Strong foundations are what allow structures to stand up to the resistance of forces externally, support heavy loads internally, and survive the tests of time eternally.

To find a structure with great stability we need look no further than the Great Pyramid of Giza in Egypt. This is the oldest and only surviving member of the Seven Wonders of the Ancient World. Strategically built over an approximately 20-year period, this awesome creation is comprised of 2.3 million blocks of stone weighing from 2.5 to 15 tons each. It is 481 feet tall, and has a foundation which covers an area of 13 square acres. The pyramid has workmanship so accurate that the four sides of the foundation have an average differential in length of only approximately 2.25 inches, and the foundation itself is horizontal and flat to within less than an inch. The sides are closely aligned to the four cardinal compass points (north, south, east, & west), which are often referred to as the Four Corners of the Earth. The Great Pyramid has endured for over 4500 years, which testifies to its external, internal, and eternal qualities. It is without a doubt a great example of deliberate plans with excellent execution that yielded great results.

I suggest we all make a paradigm shift in our success from the mediocre climbing of a ladder to the extraordinary constructing of a pyramid. As architects of our own Great Pyramid, we have the ability to construct a pyramid of success so we can achieve our intended results. *The Success Pyramid*™ below follows a well-designed blueprint. It's critical that we utilize sturdy materials to lay the foundation. Additionally, a specific pattern must be followed in solidly constructing successive layers to the top. That design allows for progressive strength and resilience while withstanding the tests of time. After the foundation is laid—and even as we are still building—we will have a much more stable structure than a ladder as we ascend to the top. There's room at all levels for multiple people. While we're developing personally we're adding the competencies that propel our progress and add strength to our structure. So unlike the "ladder climbers", we're not only ascending, but building our own success at every level—including the top. The saying "it's lonely at the top" is only indicative of ladder climbers, not pyramid builders. While constructing success, a pyramid is much stronger than a ladder.

"While constructing success, a pyramid is much stronger than a ladder."

The bonding material of the Success Pyramid is formed with relationships. They will exist within a well-designed plan for a lifetime. Additionally, new people will be introduced at every level who may play a part in the building and ascending process. As the competencies continue to develop for all, there will be no limitations to anyone's success. Neither the structure nor other people will impede progress. We will be "lifting as we climb."

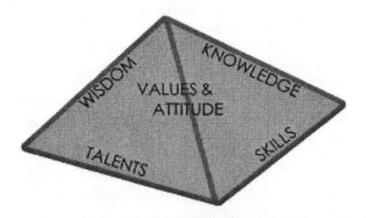

The Success Pyramid

- **The Mortar** of the pyramid is formed with our relationships. Associations we form with other people will impact our lives to some degree regardless of the nature of the relationship.

Therefore, it's imperative that those people who help support the foundation of our lives be complementary. Whether business associates, friends, family members, or lovers, we want people in our lives who are working with us, and not against us. Strength exists in numbers, and the numbers are stronger when united.

People possess varying degrees of innate talents and developed skills. Although great attributes, these aren't primary to building reciprocally beneficial alliances. The work ethic of the individuals to actually put their abilities into practice is much more important. I remember my favorite position coach in the NFL, Herm Edwards, often stated "Men, it's not just the skill, you must have the will!"—indicative of truly successful people. Those with an enduring passion to put in the extraordinary effort it takes to get the job done are the people to have on our teams. Along my life's journey I've experienced four general categories of teammates:

1. More Skill : More Will
2. Less Skill : More Will
3. More Skill: Less Will
4. Less Skill : Less Will

Category #1 is of course the ideal. These are the people who oftentimes make the biggest impacts. However, the uncommon talent and commitment of top tier performers makes it illogical to attempt to build a network exclusive to this category. Besides, I've also found Category #2 to be extremely productive. Work ethic is a character trait of the type of people we want on our teams regardless of the level of abilities they possess. The fact is, skills can be taught and talent improved. Then there's Category #3. Far too often I have seen members of this group get a pass for lack of production based on their "potential" to produce. I personally deliver no such passes. It's a much better use of time to teach someone less talented who's willing to learn and work to get better. There's a famous idiom, "you can lead a horse to water, but you can't make it drink." My spin for the quandary of this group is "you can lead a fast racehorse to the track, but you can't make it run!" Lastly there's Category #4, who we often see bouncing from job to job and relationship to relationship their entire lives. It really doesn't take long to figure out who they are. Deficient ability and work ethic negates this group's ability to even utilize the infamous "fake it til you make it" philosophy. These are the last people we would want on our teams.

The "Lifting as we Climb" philosophy applies to every member of the team. Never get caught up in pulling someone up your pyramid at an effort beyond which they are willing to climb. It's important to pick the right people for our construction teams. When they're working with us to formulate shared plans of success, it is a much more viable journey. And because successes are shared, maintaining them is more likely. TEAM (Together Everyone Achieves More) accomplishments celebrate togetherness, while individual achievements stand alone.

" . . . it's not just the skill, you must have the will!"
-Herm Edwards, former NFL Coach

- **The Four Sides**

    1. Wisdom—Acquired from both our individual experiences, as well as through life-lessons shared by others. Often packaged as common sense, wisdom when exercised properly assists us in making proper decisions. It affords us the ability to accurately weigh the consequences of our choices with their relative risks.
    2. Knowledge—Is acquired either by formal education, or informally through the introduction of new information and ideas from external sources. Our journey is propelled by our ability to apply this acquired knowledge appropriately to practical tasks.
    3. Talent* Our innate, natural abilities allow us the chance to execute specific skills at higher levels of proficiency. Examples are athletic prowess and the ability to sing in tune.
    4. Skills* Skills are abilities that can be taught and developed. Examples include typing, driving a car, and juggling.

* Both talent and skill can be improved through consistent practice. The level of proficiency we develop will be determined by our inherent level of talent, the quality of training we undertake to improve, and our commitment to systematic practice. High level performers are

those who have these abilities working in concert. An example is a professional race car driver. The skill to drive a car is an acquired ability. However, driving a race car on a fast track requires natural talent, including extremely quick muscle responses.

- **The Foundation & Core**

The basis of stability for any endeavor is its foundation. The foundation and core of the pyramid contain those elements that represent our personal foundation and core as well:

1. Our Values will often be the source of our resolve to persevere past opposition and through challenges. Our values are the things that inspire us: our Faith belief system, the love of Family and Friends, the accumulation of our Fortune, the Fun we have in our leisure time, and the recognition and accolades we receive through our Fame. We hold true to that which we genuinely believe and value. If we relate a task to our core values, we will find a way to get it done.

2. "Our Attitude determines our aptitude" is one of the simple truths of life. The enthusiasm with which we approach any given task—or life in general—will certainly impact the level of success we'll reach. The mind is an extremely strong and vital instrument. Positive thoughts lead to positive results. Negative thoughts lead to negative results. It's that simple. (I've included a great illustration in the Appendices of the value of the attitude as well. Here we place an ascending value from 1-26 on each letter from A to Z and look individually at the value of the terms on the Four Sides of The Success Pyramid. None will get you to 100%, but our core Attitude will.)

"The basis of stability for any endeavor is its foundation."

With all of the components of the Success Pyramid coming together, Success is molded and enjoyed throughout the construction. The relationships that we've formed along the way will hold the structure together soundly. Keeping an excellent Attitude and being true to our own Values insures a consistent core. While perpetually developing Wisdom, Knowledge, Talent, and Skills serves to make our success persevere for a lifetime..

Inspirations lead to Aspirations

Chapter 22

The P⁵ Principle™

I learned very early in life to prepare for (not just wish for) success. The question was asked many times during my childhood "what would (I) like to be when I grow up?" Even in my youth I had the foresight to respond "I'm going to be a professional football player and own my own business." This optimistic prediction was fueled by the faith I had in God, and by my preparations. To perform well in anything, just utilize what I call the **P⁵ Principle™** during your processes: Proper Preparation Promotes Peak Performance. I've always found it a bit interesting when people inappropriately label a confident, successful individual as conceited or cocky. All who are successful at anything had to exhibit a high degree of confidence in being able to get things done in both preparation and execution. This is not to suggest that one should be boastful. However, I've certainly observed a consistent trait in highly successful people that's not common to the masses: the confidence in their general presentation, regardless of the forum. I cover the proper use of this confidence a bit more in-depth in *The Fallacy of Humility* chapter. I call it the "It" factor. I don't believe anyone has definitively categorized what "It" is. "It" may be displayed in many different ways. But, when someone has "It", we usually take notice. When we're properly equipped and prepared for life, there's absolutely nothing wrong with sharing "It." Living within ones passion and building great relationships—while maximizing our individual talents and skills—are great building blocks for "It."

Chapter 23

$\mathscr{P}$lan to T.R.A.P. Success™

Each of us becomes what we are equipped for and prepare to be, which is not necessarily what we'd like to become (unless, of course, the two match). Success happens not by chance, but by design. And life is not lived in procedures, but in processes. One such process is a ***Plan to T.R.A.P. Success***™:

- The **T** is for **Tangible**. It is imperative with each objective we desire to achieve that we formulate a written or recorded reference. Most are familiar with the phrase "If you fail to plan, then you plan to fail." Not only does this become the road map of what to do and how to do it, but it also holds us accountable to finish the activities we start. Specific objectives must be written within a detailed plan of executing the steps to achieving them. Writing them down makes them real and tangible!

- The **R** is for **Reaching**. When given a task, our natural inclination even with the best of intentions is to complete the task if only normal obstacles are presented. Conversely, if unusual barriers are introduced, we'll perform the task up to the point of discomfort or extreme difficulty. Many of us will consider these barriers as breaking points and discontinue the task altogether. This prevents reaching excellence. Excellence perseveres through discomfort. We must condition ourselves in this unnatural work ethic for it to become our new norm. So to be successful we must reach for activities that take us beyond our comfort zones. Life was never meant to be filled with easy choices . . . If we don't risk something; we won't accomplish anything!

- The **A** is for **Applicable**. Plans should be based on useful facts, not opinions. Successful lives are lived on principles. That means what was applicable to yesterday is so today, and will be tomorrow. We can draw relevant and accurate information from many proven resources to develop our own plans.

  Once we have accurate information, we must be able to apply it practically. This can only be done if we are appropriately aligning our gifts with what we choose to do. Make sure that our activities are consistent with our natural talents and with what we plan to accomplish. We should identify our talents and passions and cultivate objectives accordingly.

- The **P** is for **Persevere**. Despite the numerous obstacles and detractors en route to achieving our goals and objectives, we must continue to execute. Positive reinforcement is great when it's available, but regardless of feedback, resilience is a must for success. Never let those who won't put in the work affect the activities of those who will! A common attribute of accomplished people is perseverance. They continued through challenges that caused many others to stop.

"It is what you do differently that makes you different."

-Bishop Dale C. Bronner

In a sermon titled "Prepare To Win", Bishop Dale C. Bronner shared the declaration "It is what you do differently that makes you different." I found this to be one of the most profound, yet simple, principles for *conditioning* to live *excellently* above uncontrollable circumstances. We each have authorship of our destiny by the free will choices we make. If we're willing to put in the time and effort necessary to commit to a plan, we will be successfully *different.* The world is guaranteed to present countless excuses for failure. Regardless of life's obstacles we still have the choice of resolve manifested through perseverance. Otherwise, timidity readily accepts mediocrity—and often, failure.

Objectives that are extremely difficult to attain are often called "wishful thinking" or "pipe dreams." It's no coincidence that wishes and dreams are constructs of closed eyes. If we plan on making them a reality, we must wake up and go do something! I am all for those who dream. But there also should be a tangible plan of actually getting things done with objectively measurable results. Otherwise the mark will be missed more often than not. Dreamers will then find themselves reminiscing about what could've been, worrying about what is, and wondering about what will be.

Excellent progress requires vision beyond our circumstances. Those who merely plan within the limiting perimeters of their valleys will never ascend to the infinite possibilities visible from mountaintops! We must recognize our talents and passions, then proactively realize our individual life's purpose. Enjoy this life, because we only have one. However, be cognizant of time spent trivially. Whatever we chose to do with our lives should be important to us first and foremost, because we're exchanging time in our lives for it.

People of excellence do things that others won't to experience the life that others don't. It should never surprise us that ordinary behaviors will never produce extraordinary results. Early 20th century politician Williams Jennings Bryan once said "Destiny is no matter of chance. It is a matter of choice. It is not a thing to be waited for, it is a thing to be achieved."

Tangible, reaching, applicable, plausible, and persevering plans of action yield successful results: the intended destiny of excellence.

Destiny is no matter of chance. It is a matter of choice. It is not a thing to be waited for, it is a thing to be achieved.

-William Jennings Bryan

Chapter 24

UPLIFT
MENTORSHIP
R.E.A.P. what you S.O.E.™

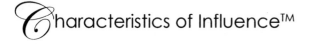

Characteristics of Influence™

Physical science and behavioral science are often not that far apart. Sir Isaac Newton's first law of motion is one example. In sum, it states that every body of mass stays in a constant state of motion (or lack of motion) unless acted upon by outside forces. Human beings intrinsically handle change the same way. Most people are extremely resistant to change. This is unfortunately true even when it's evident the change would make a particular situation better. We tend to get into comfort zones in activities and relationships. When this happens we become robotic. Ours lives end up being like the movie "Ground Hog Day": we repeat the same series of events every day.

This can certainly lead to boredom. But more importantly, it causes complacency. We must be content, not complacent. Contentment is evidenced by joy along every level of our life's journey while persevering with full effort, whereas complacency is satisfied with whatever degree of attainment and stops. When we accept a state of complacency, we cease growing and developing. At best we remain stagnant. But, with the world ever evolving around us, we often end up in a state of regression. This is supremely detrimental as it relates to our relationships. Complacency in relationships will not only stop their growth, but will often cause the people in them to drift apart. In order to ward off the negative repercussions of this behavioral flaw we must intentionally inject things that cause us to continually develop (personally and professionally).

Regardless of the type of relationship the ability to influence has the same characteristics: **Concern, Connection, Confidence, Competence, and Commitment**. If the stagnant or regressing individual does not relate positively to the entity attempting to enact change, then change will not occur. They must not be stripped of their dignity. *Change agents* must find a way to share the right information with people without making them feel like they are wrong.

All of our relationships and activities will measure the impact we personally have on others and they on us—whether positive or negative. The first gauge of whether or not there will be effective influence is the presence of genuine concern or empathy. There are situations where sympathy is needed, for example, the times when a crying friend just needs a shoulder. However, the expression of concern needed to influence change in others is empathy. When someone brings an issue to our attention, it's best that we first put ourselves in their shoes within their situation before answering any questions or making any suggestions. Our perspective on a particular subject matters only if we actually have a relevant one. We are all products of our own experiences. However, when we decide to join with others in a work environment or personal relationship, then we also open ourselves to share the experiences and perspectives of others. We will only be viewed as a trusted adviser if we're willing to put aside our own biases and predispositions before offering analysis or advice.

Shared familiarity with the activities required to successfully complete a task indicates our connection. When we are sharing ideas with others, they are best received when there is personal commonality. Whether we are receiving or giving instructions, the best delivery is by example. Likewise, the more difficult the activity, the more a personal connection to it plays a role in your ability to influence others to do it. Theory only goes so far. At some point people need to see the theory manifested before their eyes. If we are the ones sharing the theory, then we can influence others to use it by successfully practicing it ourselves. I would definitely rather see a sermon than hear one. As the old saying goes, "Practice what you preach!"

Confidence is a trait present in anyone who will accomplish—or has ever accomplished—anything significant. It's also a must if we expect to influence others to action involving change. No one wants to follow anyone who doesn't appear to have a high degree of confidence in what they are sharing.

We are able to display and observe confidence in many ways. It's evident in our speech, our walk, our posture, our expressions, and of course our results. There is certainly a fine line between extreme confidence and cockiness. But if ever there were an appropriate time to walk right up to that line, that moment when we want to convince someone to make a life altering change is it. Can you imagine an army general leading his troops into battle displaying a lack of confidence? Well, neither can I. Nor can I imagine any soldiers following a general who lacks confidence into battle. This analogy works in our everyday lives as well. Our co-workers, spouses, children, other family members, and teammates need to sense confidence in us to whatever degree we expect to influence them. In order for others to accept our advice as truth it is best that we become a proven example first!

Competence in the knowledge necessary to execute our activities is essential. This is the one "Characteristic of Influence" that serves as a basis for all the others. I've witnessed a number of people stumbling through presentations in which they were tasked to influence change, during which I could see the glazed-over eyes of the audience. I knew then that nothing was going to happen any differently for those participants—they weren't going to change at all. Conversely, I've observed presentations in which the presenter was very well-versed in the subject matter. Their delivery demonstrated concern for members of the audience, a connection to the processes they shared, confidence that the principles work, and a commitment to professionally and effectively delivering the information.

"The difference between a successful person and others is not a lack of strength, not a lack of knowledge, but rather a lack of will."
—Vince Lombardi

Commitment is the most self-explanatory of the influences. Like competence, this "Characteristic of Influence" is closely connected with the other four. Without the will to finish what we start, our skills and competencies don't matter. Another famous quote from Vince Lombardi speaks to the relativity of this trait to success: "The difference between a successful person and others is not a lack of strength, not a lack of knowledge, but rather a lack of will." When you are committed, you demonstrate the perseverance to complete that task in which you also show Concern for others, a Connection to having done it yourself, Confidence in the results it produces, and demonstrated Competence in your knowledge and performance. Collectively, the result is a credible influence for change.

Dr. Martin Luther King, Jr. was an effective Change Agent

Chapter 25

T.E.A.M.: A Winning Model

We should always be *lifting as we climb* on our life's journeys. Our ability to thrive hinges on our ability to accept whatever role we may have as a member of a team. If we're a success, then it's likely that a successful group of people surrounds us.

Winning teams have a commonality. They are united in their objectives and in the processes necessary to achieve them. Prospective team members must possess the talent, dedication, and work ethic it takes to complete the individual duties of assigned roles.

Personnel decisions at all levels are based upon matching properly skilled candidates with available positions. When these decisions are made properly, and team members are working to their full potential, excellence in results will be achieved.

Professional sports teams have developed multi-million-dollar Personnel and Operations departments that focus on mastering the selection and development areas of workforce quality control. These organizations assemble the world's elite athletes to perform for the entertainment of millions of fans. The ultimate measure of success for these sports operations is the annual crowning of a single world champion in each sport. Every year, this "Champions Way" is what teams strive once again to emulate.

A winning individual or organizational reputation is the most recognizable asset on our path to the "Champions Circle". An exemplary reputation is not only a draw for those looking to receive from you, but also for individuals or organizations wanting to associate with you. Remember that nothing great is accomplished in solitude! **Together Everyone Achieves More.** This is the essence of teamwork. As a team, however, there are still ways to improve both organizationally and individually. If being the best is your objective then unity within consistently executed systems is a must.

The "Champions Way" as executed by elite level professional athletes is a great example of how excellent processes yield notable results. Although known for being the best in the world at what they do, athletes on professional sports teams prepare for their competitions as if they're mere novices. There are countless hours of research, scouting, meetings, film study, fitness training, and practices in preparation to deliver a performance that lasts for only a few hours at most. The predominant attitude of this unique group of people is that winning is the only acceptable culmination of their work. The high performers have a philosophy applicable to all who value success: a commitment to tenacious preparation, and excellent execution of all tasks of their profession.

Teamwork

Chapter 26

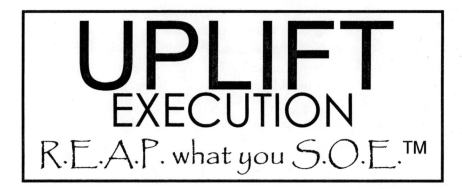

"Unity in purpose yields the greatest results".

$\mathcal{P}$.R.O. R.E.A.L.M. Execution™

As stated previously, the concepts within this book are designed to help lead you to UPLIFT. This is ultimately achieved when elite performers are collectively assembled as TEAMs executing tasks to accomplish the same objectives. Unity in purpose yields the greatest results.

The key components of excellence cultivated in winning sports organizations are transferable to building winning TEAMs within any area of our lives. I've formulated the acronym P.R.O. R.E.A.L.M. to capture the systems professional athletes use to condition themselves to consistently execute excellence. In other words, they're relentlessly conditioning themselves to reach new and higher-level comfort zones all the time:

- **P**ractical—Match the skill-set of the individual to the task at hand. So, we should be sure that the processes we utilize and the skills we possess are applicable to our planned tasks or careers. We must be aware of our own natural talents and skills. Additionally, we should be cognizant of our areas of weakness. I often utilize the doubts of my detractors as motivation—as do most driven individuals. Never should we allow someone else to decide what we can or can't accomplish. However, part of our consistent growth entails developing a keen self-awareness of our own strengths and weaknesses. A critic's negativity is powerless when we're already well aware of our own potential. But, it's up to us to align our gifts with their appropriate calling. Intellectual acumen tells us what we should do, but wisdom actually does it.

- **R**elational—It is extremely important that you develop quality interpersonal communication and relationships. We must have a since of relativity with the other members of our teams or groups. And we ourselves must be able to communicate clearly and effectively. We should all make sure that we speak, read, and write the language(s) used within our networks proficiently. And we should also clearly define terms with usages unique to our teams or groups.

My mom used to tell us some great stories when we were young. One was about Tom, the town wino where she grew up. Tom was actually well-liked by the town folks; he would hitch rides with various people to get around. Well, one day the pastor of the town church was giving Tom a ride when they came to a stop sign. The Pastor looked his way and asked Tom if a car was coming from Tom's direction. Tom said no, and the pastor proceeded to pull out into the intersection. After the loud screeching of brakes and the avoidance of what could have been a horrible accident, the pastor looked over at Tom and said, "I thought you said that there was no car coming!" Tom, with a straight face, said, "That wasn't no car, that was a TRUCK!" We've shared many laughs with this story over the years. But it serves as a great example of why it's important to relate and communicate with other individuals effectively. It can be the difference between success or failure—or in the case of Tom and the pastor, it could have been the difference between life and death.

- **O**rganized—Prepare a readily available and tangible plan of operating procedures. As we discussed previously, "TRAP" success with a plan that specifies responsibilities, schedules and time lines for completion.

- **R**eliable—Always provide your team with truthful information. Use strategies, techniques, and processes from credible sources. It's often said that there's nothing new under the sun. So within whatever field we venture, there are likely to be references for success from which we can draw inferences. Then we have the ability to take those facts and possibly improve upon them. There's no reason to reinvent a wheel that has proven to roll already. We can just make it roll faster and more efficiently.

- **E**xperiential-Consistently and persistently practice your tasks. We need to have continuous hands-on practice at whatever it is we plan to do excellently. No matter how good our natural skills are, we must practice in order for them to be great—and with practice, they can always become better. We should never feel that we have arrived, because no matter how successful we are, there is always room for improvement.

As the founder of Microsoft, Bill Gates has amassed a fortune so large that generations of people following him won't be able to spend it. Yet from 1975 when he and his childhood friend started the company, until 2008, he diligently went to work just like any other employee to improve his product. In July, 2008 he finally transitioned out of a day-to-day role in the company to spend more time on global health and education through his foundation. This serves as a great segue to our next letter . . .

- **A**ccountable—Make sure you have one or more accountability partners to help hold you to the tangible plan. These individuals should have access to your plan. Make an agreement with them to check in with you periodically or through a scheduled follow. The purpose is to gauge your progression through, and adherence to, the planned activities. Regardless of the level of discipline we have individually, strength is better in numbers. And encouragement from others is helpful in persevering through challenges.

Personal fitness trainers are great examples of accountability partners. Successful workout programs alone are easily accessible with little or no expense. However, having an individual who pushes us to be our best has value. The human element of feedback, with encouragement and critique, helps us overcome seemingly insurmountable obstacles.

I have put together an accountability group of close friends with whom I hold a weekly conference call. We meet for an hour to discuss our objectives for the year (personal, familial, spiritual, and professional). Each of us rotates weeks to share our current activities. We provide one another with candid feedback: including offering helpful ideas, sharing constructive criticism, and giving genuine encouragement.

- **L**ateral—Share information at the level of the recipient. We should never speak down to a teammate, or act as if a task being asked of someone else is beneath us. I was able to experience a very practical example of this by one of my most respected leaders. My high school football coach, the late Lee Forehand, was quite the character. His favorite word was *intensity*, and he had a saying that we would conduct practice "whether rain, shine, sleet, snow, or volcano."

This saying was just a joke to us until the day we met a torrential storm of unseasonably cold rain during spring practice. The majority of the team was dragging through the beginning of practice. We couldn't believe we were really practicing in such bad weather. It's just not supposed to get that cold in the spring in Georgia.

Initially Coach Forehand appeared to just patiently empathize with our plight. He stood calmly with his trademark fisherman's hat tilted to the side while chewing on a toothpick. After approximately 10 minutes, though, he had had enough. He gathered us in the middle of the field to form a huddle around him. After we were all in place he *took off* running towards the biggest puddle of water and mud he could find and did a huge belly-flop into it. When he arose, without his hat, and completely covered in who knows what, his next statements were, *"Are we ready to practice now?"*and *"Where's my hat?"*

We were all initially in a state of shock, and a bit amused. But, with this he changed the entire mood of the team. We were inspired by his actions (and somewhat moved to insanity)! We proceeded to do our best imitations of his belly-flop in various mud puddles throughout the practice field. After we recovered his hat, what followed was the best practice in which I had ever participated. As extreme as it may have been, he came to our level and led by example to get us into the right mind frame to be excellent. We were all wet, cold, and muddy. But the right mental disposition overcame the conditions. And as our leader Coach Forehand demonstrated that it wasn't beneath him to join us.

- **Measurable**—Establish clearly defined objectives in which you can quantify success. Our objectives should always have a definite gauge for their successful completion—one that is not subject to opinion. There is a reason we keep a numerical score in sporting events. The scoreboard will always reveal which team has won, or which teams have tied. From a personal perspective, we must make sure we define what success means to us. Therein we know for certain when we've achieved it. We should never let another person's opinion define our success . . . and we should never let anyone tell us what we can't accomplish. That's why it's important to set specific objectives, and not just vague goals.

Be deliberate as you construct your winning team. Choose team members who have the natural talents and developed skill sets applicable to the tasks expected of them. After your team members are selected, your collective ability to manage quality interpersonal communication is of the utmost importance. This is especially true for the leader. Leaders must lead by example and make available to the team members a written or recorded reference with proven successful tactics to achieve the desired objectives. Leaders will be found throughout Success Pyramids, but nowhere along a ladder is there even one. An absolute necessity of leadership is the ability to lift others to higher levels while self-developing as well. This only takes place with people operating on the same levels.

Each person's perception of accomplishment is his reality, regardless of what other people think. For altruism to exist, one must discern the needs of his/ her constituents by being a great listener and collaborator. If we are unable to relate a task to the since of accomplishment as seen through the eyes of the person executing that task, we will not get the best results possible.

We all schedule time in our lives for what we value. If it's important to us, we will find a way to get it done. So, the most effective way to ensure success within a team environment is to relate desired organizational objectives to agreed upon individual objectives. The objectives must be quantifiable. This removes the possibility of a subjective opinion of success, and builds team trust in the unity of purpose. Winning teams have all of the above components. What about yours?

1993 Green Bay Packers

Chapter 27

The Fallacy of Humility™

It's become common in acceptance speeches and awards ceremonies for the winners to share how *humbled* they are to receive such an honor. As a believer in Jesus Christ, I recognize the place for humility, particularly as it relates to recognizing the role of my Lord and Savior in all that I'm able to experience. However, I've also never been one for following traditions just for traditions sake and making baseless trivial statements. To be humbled means to be made ordinary, meek, modest, lowly, or unassuming. Conversely, when one is being honored it is exalting, not humbling. When exalted s/he is recognized as extraordinary, while being praised or acclaimed. I think it's time we stop pretending that extraordinary people, producing extraordinary results, are just like everyone else. They are not! The preparation is not ordinary, nor is the execution ordinary. Therefore the results are not ordinary. Life presents various opportunities for us all. However, if extraordinary achievements are in our plans, then we must be committed to putting in the dedicated effort it takes to produce at that level. Not everyone is willing to do this.

"The winners of life's races are almost certain to be those who approach the beginning, middle, and end of them highly confident in their abilities, and extremely passionate about executing them."

Each of our lives can be viewed as a race in which some manner of equality exists only at the starting line. Then it's up to the individual to pick the proper race to run in order to perform to the best of our abilities. Thereafter we must plan our strategies, train ourselves holistically, and then *run* as fast and efficiently as possible to the finish line. Recognizing the top finishers of each *race* should be viewed favorably. This is the result to which we aspire. The winners of life's races are almost certain to be those who approach the beginning, middle, and end of them highly confident in their abilities, and extremely passionate about executing them. I remember a number of my coaches in the NFL sharing a similar ideology about football. They stated that we won't all be treated the same, but we will be treated fairly. Obviously it would not be fair for a player of superior talent to share equal playing time with his less talented backup just because they're on the same team. No manner of real life works that way. And we should cease nurturing such entitlement in our kids through the current structure of most youth sports programs in America. We must nurture the excellent work ethic during the formidable years, because in adulthood the race will be won by s/he who is able to endure the longest at the highest levels.

I often find it amusing watching broadcasts of sporting events. It has become common-place for some analysts to point out the *humility* of the players who make a huge play or score without any signs of exhilaration. Conversely, those who show any degree of excitement or celebration are viewed as arrogant, boastful, or selfish. The critique repeated most for the "celebrators" is they should "act like they've been there before!" Ironically this advice is often being given by those who've never been there before (never played the sport at a high level). In the case of an ex-player giving color commentary, I don't know if they're just doing their jobs, or if somehow they've forgotten what it was like to be there.

I actually wonder what these same announcers feel about their peers who actually appear to execute their craft with a similar excitement as the aforementioned "celebrator" athletes. Does "acting like they've been there before" in this case mean the announcers should call the third and final strike of a no hitter the same way they call the third and final strike of the first inning? I don't think so! So who decides what is worthy of our excitement and passion? Both the athletes and the announcers are involved in the entertainment industry. And the celebratory athletes, along with the excitable announcers are who I and many others find to be most entertaining.

Most athletes are conditioned from the moment they began playing in youth leagues to be confident in their ability, have fun, be enthusiastic, and give their all. Of course as these athletes matriculate through the levels of competition, there's a sifting of the pool. This takes place for a number of reasons including levels of talent, changes in interests, and unforeseen injuries. It's highly likely though when referencing the athletes who have made it to the higher levels of their respective sports, that they have experienced and adopted a fun, enthusiastic, and high effort approach. During this process they have also become well aware and confident of their particular areas of talent. This is not only indicative of competition day. The training necessary to be high performing athletes also requires a high level of enthusiasm and effort to complete. Additionally, the level of difficulty is such that if fun is not injected into the mix somehow, then the regimens would grow old really early in the process and the athletes will burn out.

"Life is also too precious and short to not enjoy the journey."

Sports are widely thought of as microcosms of life. There are plans, responsibilities, execution, expectations, failures, accomplishments, and more. Life is also too precious and short to not enjoy the journey. Just as in sports, in life there should be an expectation of some form of merriment to follow accomplishments. Of course, there's also appropriate etiquette relative to the environment. So, I'd certainly expect a different display of enthusiasm for a win in a courtroom than I would on a basketball court. But, the point is it would be expected.

After years of involvement in team sports, and the types of extraordinary preparation it takes to compete in them, it's almost heresy to expect athletes to not display a high degree of confidence and passion in executing their crafts. And without a full sense of relativity and perspective for the challenges of preparing for and executing a particular skill, it's hard to have a truly relevant opinion anyway. Even as an athlete, there is no way I could critique the appropriate pre-race display of confidence for a marathon; or the way to celebrate progressing through or finishing it. I have no experiential perspective. However, I do know that it must take extraordinary physical conditioning and execution. So however the participants choose to rejoice during or following a race, I say go for it as long as it doesn't degrade others.

Athletes, just like business owners, corporate executives, doctors, lawyers or any other person living out their calling, will be elated with their successes naturally. The unnatural response would be the opposite: to just act as if what you just accomplished was no big deal, and happens anytime to anybody. Well, it is a big deal and it doesn't just happen! The individuals and teams who are accomplishing the "victories" of life whether in the board room, on the playing fields, on operating tables, or court rooms have set themselves apart, and put in the work it takes to get there.

Humility has its place, but it's highly doubtful that you'll find it authentically at the victory podium. There is an apropos quote by British novelist Jane Austen in *Pride and Prejudice*, "Nothing is more deceitful than the appearance of humility. It is often only carelessness of opinion, and sometimes an indirect boast." Those judgmental comments by television commentators are more careless than the celebrations are.

"Once a king, always a king"
-Ron Springs

One of my most outspoken coaches, the late Ron Springs (formerly of the Dallas Cowboys) use to often use the idiom "Once a king, always a king" when referencing the confidence with which we should carry ourselves and live our lives. Carrying ones head high does not insinuate that others should carry theirs low. Meekness, insignificance, lowness, and submissiveness are never terms associated with efforts being summoned from those expected to bring home the victory, close a business deal, or deliver a convincing closing argument. What we expect to see is extreme confidence, tenacity, passion, and excitement.

" . . . instead of giving the high achievers recognition of a position to which others should hope to ascend, many of our current systems offer up the fallacy of humility as if everyone is performing on the same level."

I have a feeling that the fallacy of humility notion was introduced by someone who couldn't relate to the conditioned enthusiasm and tenacity of high performers. They didn't understand the "It" factor, or how to get "It". So, in the politically correct society in which we now live, they have to level the playing field so lesser performers aren't made to feel bad because they don't have "It". Unfortunately, as has become the case for youth sports, this has now started to show up in our school systems. In youth sports, trophy ceremonies for merely participating have become the norm. And some schools don't openly recognize honors students as to not alienate the others. So instead of giving the high achievers recognition of a position to which others should hope to ascend, many of our current systems offer up the fallacy of humility as if everyone is performing on the same level. I'd venture to guess that is not how things are done in Singapore where their students lead the world in nearly every academic measure of testing. They certainly understand what "It" is, and the commitment and effort it takes to acquire "It".

One of the joys of my post-playing football career has been coaching and training young athletes. I was known for the passion and tenacity with which I played the game. Those traits continued in coaching, and often transferred to my players. Every team and sports camp in which this was the atmosphere, the kids and parents shared that it provided the most fun and most development they'd experienced. So challenging lessons and training administered via enthusiastic instruction is actually viewed as something enjoyable! What a novel concept!

In the spring of 2005 I was blessed with the opportunity to lead a football team of young men in Arizona through a very special season. My fellow coaches, along with the families and friends of the players, rode the wave of enthusiasm, tenacity, and fun along with us the entire season. We did so all the way to the State Championship. From the inception of that program our philosophy was shared with the parents and players:

> *We give glory to our Lord and Savior Jesus Christ. We will pray at every practice and game. If this offends you then you should find another organization to join. We are a competitive football team whose objective is to cultivate excellence in our players. This excellence is defined as doing the best we can with what we've got. We WILL win . . . We will Succeed . . . "Winning/ Success" results from individual player and team development to full potential. These achievements constitute residual effects of the progression through processes. In whatever you do, do it with enthusiasm!"*

"Our humility was in recognizing the importance of our teamwork and unity, not in fabricating some false sense of meekness in what we accomplished."

Every member of our organization believed in the philosophy. We prepared, practiced, and played the same way all the time. It was a challenging but rewarding atmosphere. We exuded enthusiasm, confidence, and class. We were the organization others talked about and wanted to join. Celebrating our success had nothing to do with pointing out the failures of others. Our humility was in recognizing the importance of our teamwork and unity, not in fabricating some false sense of meekness in what we accomplished. That fallacy had no place at the celebration of our championship. We had accomplished the extraordinary and been set apart. I wanted everyone to enjoy that feeling, and understand the type of passion, commitment, and effort it took to get there so they each can replicate it in other areas of their lives for the rest of their lives.

I'm all for humility when used in its correct context. In accomplishments introduce it as a trait of individuals who recognize with whom to share credit, and do so without degrading their competition. And in challenges where we are truly humbled by a task or challenge superior to our abilities then be self aware enough to admit it. I've had my fair share of both instances of its proper use. There's no appropriate occasion for either boasting or mocking competitors either way. But, we should also not associate the confidence and enthusiasm displayed in accomplishments with belittling others. Nor should it be equated to a lack of respect for one's craft. Conversely, it's an outpouring of the culmination of the work of the special few who have made extraordinary investments to reach extraordinary outcomes. Can you imagine the builders of the Great Pyramid of Giza doing so timidly? As colossal a challenge as it must have been, I imagine the architects, engineers, and workers, were all confident it would be done and had to execute it enthusiastically. And I'll bet the celebration that took place at its completion was legendary!

Kansas City Chiefs—1993

Chapter 28

UPLIFT
BALANCE
R.E.A.P. what you S.O.E.™

"Even with correctly aligned inspirations, gifts, and aspirations . . . we must also have balance."

 alanced Plans

Success, although rewarding, has its share of challenges. It's said that even too much of a good thing is bad. That can certainly be the case for those of us who have a tenacious internal drive to succeed. Even with correctly aligned inspirations, gifts, and aspirations, we must also have balance in our lives. And regardless of our individual strengths and passion, we are each still subject to human frailty.

A couple of years ago I was struck by an interesting health research finding: the most common day for heart attacks is Monday. Specifically on Monday mornings, heart attacks spike between 4 a.m. and 10 a.m. more than any other six-hour period of the week.1 For most adults, this time of day is preparation for work. So, some people are literally dying to miss work. It might be an over-generalization to blame all of these Monday morning heart attacks on the impending work day. However, common sense suggests that it's at least contributory.

The research also found that heart attacks can be triggered by stress or emotional upset. One of the famous quotes by Confucius is "Choose a job you love and you'll never work a day in your life." Unfortunately, most things we view as work also cause us a degree of stress. In work situations I've observed some people overwhelmed by, or unprepared for, a particular assignment; some who are doing a job just for the paycheck; and some who are overworked regardless of their love for what they are doing. I surmise that many heart attack victims probably didn't heed Confucius' advice. Many working people need more balance.

1Maloof, Rich: Monday Morning Heart Attacks . . . and Other Health Risks by the Day of the Week . . . The associations between your health and the days of the week. MSN Health & Fitness. 2009.

"Choose a job you love and you'll never work a day in your life."
-Confucius

Balance usually refers to a balance between work and life. To stay consistent in avoiding traditionally-used and/or negative terms, I'm introducing the term professional/personal balance. Work/life insinuates that our profession is not a part of our lives. That in itself makes work a negative. If we're not living when we're working, then how would we ever enjoy work?

Our lives do include work, play, rest, and any other activity we choose. But we should never be so heavily invested in any one area that the others are neglected. If our professional life is unbalanced the stresses can add up and make us more likely to be a Monday morning heart attack statistic.

Conversely, if we're overly involved in personal matters then it's doubtful that our professional responsibilities are being fully met.

Additional considerations in balancing our personal lives are leisure activities, health and fitness, and rest. When we look at how the human biological clock works there is rather convincing evidence of divine design. We just must listen to our bodies if we would like to get maximal production from them. Each day with which we're blessed is twenty-four hours long. There's nothing we can do to add or take away from its length. We can only control how we manage an infinite array of possible activities in this finite time frame. The traditional workday is eight hours long, and it's generally recommended that adults get an average of eight hours of sleep a night. This strongly suggests an easy solution to the needed balance. There are basically three areas in which we divide our time: work, personal activities, and sleep. If we heed the times that should be allotted to work and sleep then we have eight hours remaining each day for personal activities. This ideal is true life balance.

I know what most people think about this ideal balance. You believe personal life uncertainties and professional life demands will not allow such an even distribution to occur. Well, even if we are unable to wholly incorporate this ideal into our personal schedule, making a proactive plan for better balance will put us closer to its achievement. Most are familiar with the phrase "If you fail to plan, then you plan to fail." The solution I came up with in my own life has been to have a proactively scheduled balanced plan. In other words within my Outlook and Blackberry calendars are scheduled professional and personal activities. Beyond customary appointments, also scheduled within my calendars are such things as changing A/C filters, calling family and friends, and buying birthday cards. Usually when I share this strategy with others the initial question I get is "What about spontaneity?" Many of these questioners lack balance in their own lives. They were themselves inconsistent in meeting the expectations of others. So to that spontaneity question I respond, "Well, how's spontaneity working for YOU?" After a brief introspection most of my clients are then willing to consider a proactively scheduled Balance Plan.

Chapter 29

ℱunctional Fitness

An area of a properly Balanced Plan that seems to cycle in and out of people's lives (like the New Year's Resolution to which it is often associated) is Health & Fitness. The body is the temple that houses the mind and the spirit. In order to perform our best physically, mentally, and spiritually, it is helpful that our bodies look, feel, and function their best. Physical exercise, combined with a properly administered balanced diet is the most efficient way of achieving these maximal benefits. Like the other areas of success, maintaining our health and fitness at optimum levels requires a strategic and consistently executed plan. A great "side effect" of a well functioning and fit body is that it also usually presents a more aesthetically pleasing appearance as well!

Thankfully for me, growing up in a home with a father whose career was in health and fitness made incorporating these truths much easier. And the advice of doctors as a result of the battering my body took over 25-years of tackle football made it a must. In order for me to avoid the lifetime of aches and pains many athletes suffer, my doctors told me that I needed to control my weight, maintain my muscle tone, and stay fit. The advice definitely makes sense to me. And as I thought about the extended quality of life it affords anyone in any occupation as we age, it made sense for everyone.

For most people who have gained excess weight over the years a slowing metabolism is much of the blame. Our basal metabolic rate (the rate at which our body uses energy) affects both our ability to maintain our weight, or shed pounds. The sedentary lifestyles of our society today only serve to exacerbate this effect. Unfortunately, the conveniences of modern technology have also been catalysts to our trending obesity. The Center for Consumer Freedom released a 2007 report that sedentary lifestyles, not diets, are leading to our obesity epidemic. The report noted that televisions now outnumber people in American households; children on average are much more involved in sitting and playing video games rather than playing outside; people use power tools like leaf blowers, and machines such as riding mowers far more than rakes or push mowers; and that women in particular have started taking on non-physically-oriented jobs in the workplace in record numbers. Balance must be injected into the lives of these individuals; or the quality of their earthly time will suffer greatly. Additionally, the assets they're working so hard to accumulate are being threatened by the costs associated with their increased need for healthcare. From ages 20 to 56 obese people have the most expensive health costs. Ironically though, because they don't live as long as their smaller counterparts, overall costs are less. I'm sure most of you, as I, will take the additional expense over the shortened life.

Chapter 30

"Why build a Success Pyramid in which unattended elements of our health and fitness predispose us to a short period of enjoyment?"

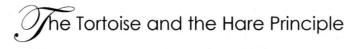e Tortoise and the Hare Principle

The number one reason people give for lack of physical activity or exercise is busy schedules. Not far behind is lack of results once they do start exercising. As a lifelong athlete, I have always had great eating and exercise habits. However, I do have perspective on the compounded difficulty of getting back into shape as opposed to maintaining a healthy and fit lifestyle. Common to executing each of the plans for cultivating success is what I call the Tortoise and the Hare Principle. This is based on Aesop's fable of the same name. In other words success will be the by-product of a consistent cultivation of our own skills and talents throughout our lives.

It will not be evidenced by sporadic periods of effort. This is no different for our health and fitness. A consistent lifestyle of moderate exercise and a balanced diet are much more sustainable than infrequent periods of fad diets and/or trendy weight loss programs. Besides, no successful person wants to be a living contradiction. Why begin building a Success Pyramid in which unattended elements of our health and fitness predispose us to a short period of construction?

Upon my retirement from football, I decided to learn much more about the physiology and biomechanics behind the body I had spent so much of my life developing. The advice of my doctors to stay fit had intrigued me beyond just controlling imminent aches and pains. It was time for me to understand why training was structured the way it was to produce the proper body composition needed for optimum performance. I certainly realized that I was first and foremost genetically blessed to respond well to training. This was evident early on, even in high school, as my muscular development responded in a relatively faster timeframe than many of my peers. However, there were still commonalities to training that I knew had to be consistent with others who have maintained a healthy weight and good fitness habits over the years. I ventured to find the universally transferrable elements of my training regimen that I could continue for the rest of my life as well as share with others. Over the years, DNA, my diet, and training had developed my body into a veritable fat burning machine. So my metabolism has actually been on overdrive for much of my life. Through my studies and personal training certification process I was able to uncover the primary controllable ingredients to this phenomenon.

There are multiple drivers that affect metabolism, some of which we can control. Age, stress, rest, exercise, diet, and overall health all play a part. We are all subject to aging as long as we're blessed to be alive. So, there is nothing we can do to stop the process. However, since we know our metabolism decreases with age, we should be even more diligent about consistent exercise to at least slow its negative impact. The earlier we institute a regular training regimen the more likely it will be maintained later. Even if we wait it's never too late to start enhancing our lifestyles. During our middle-aged years we should establish a workout plan to which we will commit to carry us into our senior years. It's critical during this time to have some form of consistent resistance training. Toned and strengthened muscles work wonders for supporting aging bones and joints. The Centers for Disease Control and Prevention suggests adults all ages 18 and up at a minimum need about two and a half hours of moderate-intensity aerobic activity each week, as well as strengthening exercises for all muscle groups twice a week.

"The Centers for Disease Control and Prevention suggests Adults all ages 18 and up at a minimum need about two and a half hours of moderate-intensity aerobic activity each week, as well as strengthening exercises for all muscle groups twice a week."

There are established connections between psychological stress and our adrenal systems. Reducing the stressors in our lives will not only ward off Monday morning heart attacks, but also aid in our weight control plans. When we have emotional pressures our bodies release cortisol, a hormone produced by the adrenal system that is linked to weight gain. Regular physical activity, deep breathing, and even professional help from a psychologist or counselor may be needed. Regardless of the methodology, it's crucial to our overall health and well-being that we tame the stressors in our lives.

Not getting sufficient sleep can significantly alter our body's processes enough to predispose us to gain weight. Lack of sleep over just one night can disrupt our metabolic patterns. This unfortunately also causes insulin resistance, which has been associated with obesity. We should get seven to nine hours of sleep each night to increase our ability to boost metabolism. Not only will we awake well rested, but also with more fat burning energy. This can be a tough discipline for extremely driven people. However, we all need to know when to say when. There comes a point in time when an extreme work ethic produces diminishing returns, particularly when the body's proper amount of rest is being compromised.

"Not getting enough sleep can significantly alter our body's processes enough to predispose us to gain weight."

Physical activities and exercise may increase our resting metabolic rate while expending more calories. We should have a regular schedule of exercise in our weekly calendars. Regardless of whether it's through a health club, local YMCA, or at home the key is to do something regularly. Also, be sure to set aside a dedicated time. Exercise is too important an element of a sustainable plan for success to just try to work in somewhere. It must be scheduled within our calendars. There are many different strategies to working out. Before beginning though, we must identify the desired outcome of our efforts. My approach has always focused on functional fitness. Whether through participation in sports or carrying out daily activities, we should be prepared to perform at our best. The group and individual fitness programs for my personal clients have been designed accordingly. I call this FAB Fitness Training (Functional Adult Bootcamp). You can request a personalized plan through my website (www.upliftsystems.com). There are many options to fit multiple fitness objectives, lifestyles, and schedules.

What I've found most useful has been a coordination of aerobic conditioning, resistance training focused on muscle confusion, and interval anaerobic training. For those able to make the time commitment these are formatted within an annual training schedule that includes three 12-week periods of strategic training (anatomical adaptation, functional improvement, & anaerobic endurance), one 14-week period of maintenance, and a 2-week period of rest. During the two week rest period, I recommend having an annual physical. It's also a good idea to detoxify the body of waste materials/toxins that have built up over the year. I recommend to my clients, and undergo myself a couple of Colon Hydrotherapy sessions and a 7-Day Detox. These help recoup and prepare body for the forthcoming year of excellence. My FAB Fitness Training workouts are normally three days a week (sometimes four) via a combination of health club and outdoor sessions. Group sessions are primarily conducted outdoors, and personal training in a health club.

Additionally, I've designed modified programs for those individuals with limited time and/or resources. Whether single parents who get very little time to themselves, or busy professionals with massive workloads, addressing health and fitness is still of the utmost importance. For these people though convenience is the key. This is the first consideration of these workouts. Each of the 30-minute sessions can be done right in the comfort of a bedroom or living room. There's also no special equipment necessary.

Whether you chose to become a FAB Fitness client or start your own fitness training program, the key is to start something. But an area of note that I've had to introduce to most of my personal clients is how to properly warm up. Warm-ups should entail activities that increase the core temperature of the body while loosening the muscles. This prepares us to properly train or perform while limiting exposure to injury. The proper pre-workout/competition warm-up will involve a short aerobic activity followed by a series of dynamic stretching movements (a video demonstration of a full warm-up can be found on my website: www.upliftsystems.com). Quite simply, if you don't have at least a light sweat at the end of your warm-ups, then you're likely NOT warmed up. The common mistake most people make is to do static stretches (those you hold in a stationary pose) before they workout or compete. This is counterproductive; as the freshly stretched muscle filaments will be weaker and more susceptible to injury. Static stretching should only be done following workouts or competitions. This helps to improve flexibility. When done properly, these stretches should be held for at least 30 seconds, up to the micro-stretching timeframe of 60 seconds per pose. The overall benefit of these changes oftentimes improves both training results and performance.

Another common misconception is that cutting our diets is the way to lose weight. Actually, not eating enough of the right foods can cause body metabolism to slow down. Biologically, improperly nourished bodies will attempt to conserve calories—counteracting the original intent of the diet reduction. Moreover, under-eating or meal-skipping can make us more likely to overeat later. The best strategy I've found is dividing our 3-meal daily calorie intake into 5 or 6 smaller meals throughout the day. It's important to make all meals. Particularly pertinent is breakfast. This is the metabolism kick start for our day. Healthy snacks and meal replacement shakes can be included as smaller meals.

I found an ideal nutritional products partner in ViSalus SCIENCES. This company has an excellent line of meal replacement shakes and natural supplements. It also created the Body by Vi™ 90-Day Challenge that has been instrumental in changing many lives. After sampling the products myself and seeing great results, I became a distributor as well to help share them with others. You can find out more about these great products on my website.

Another dietary essential to weight control is a healthy water intake. I've always utilized the bodyweight approach by dividing bodyweight by two and converting that figure to ounces for the amount of daily water intake. The Institute of Medicine—which was formed to provide national advice on issues relating to biomedical science, medicine, and health—advises that men consume roughly 13 cups of total beverages a day and women consume about 9 cups. Whichever method you incorporate, you'll find an increased water intake supremely beneficial. In addition to assisting with weight control, proper water intake also flushes toxins out of vital organs, carries nutrients to your cells and provides a moist environment for ear, nose and throat tissues. The last crucial element of the daily diet is to never eat or drink anything except water after 9PM or 2 hours before bedtime, whichever is earlier.

As always, check with a physician for medical clearance before beginning any health and fitness program. When you're cleared, be sure to execute your physical training with the same excellent approach as other areas of your life. Most people can get a hold of weight problems with a consistent plan, and proper eating habits. In some rare situations, problems like hypothyroidism or low testosterone levels (in men) can cause body functions to slow down and uncontrollable weight gain to result. In both cases medications are available. An ideal training plan is physically challenging, while keeping us mentally focused. This provides another excellent element of a well balanced life of success. If we take into consideration the dedication and effort it takes to structure our Pyramids of Success, we should do everything possible to extend our mortal time enjoying them!

Phase I—Anatomical Adaptation

Warm-up	**Weeks 1 through 3**
Stationary Bike/Elliptical	5-minutes
Dynamic Stretch	10X's Each Movement

1)Neck Rotations, 2)Arm Rotations, 3)Trunk Rotations 4)Knee Rotations 5)Ankle Rotations 6)Walking High Knees 7)Walking Toe Touches 8)Lateral Leg Swings 9)Anterior/Posterior Leg Swings 10)Calf Raises/Stretches

Workout: Perform 3-Circuits of the exercises with bodyweight or dumbbells where possible. You have 30-secs. of work and 30 secs. To get to the next station and begin. You have 2-mins. Rest at the completion of a cycle.

Exercises	**Repetitions***
1. **90 Degree Squat**	30 seconds
2. Push-ups	30 seconds
3. Walking Lunges	30 seconds
4. Seated Core Twists	30 seconds
5. Narrow Stance Push-ups	30 seconds
6. Swiss Ball Crunches	30 seconds
7. Superman	30 seconds
8. Dumbbell Overhead Presses	30 seconds
9. Calf Raises	30 seconds
10. Lateral Walking Lunges	30 seconds

Conditioning:

Anaerobic Conditioning-	10 x 20yds. Ladders (30—Seconds rest in between each)
Micro-Stretching	**Hold each stretch 40-60 Secs.**

Sample FAB Fitness weekly workout—Monday

*Each exercise is done for the maximum repetitions possible at your own pace during the time designated.

Phase I—Anatomical Adaptation

Warm-up	**Weeks1 through 3**
Stationary Bike/Elliptical	5-minutes
Dynamic Stretch	10X's Each Movement

1)Neck Rotations, **2)**Arm Rotations, **3)**Trunk Rotations **4)**Knee Rotations **5)**Ankle Rotations **6)**Walking High Knees **7)**Walking Toe Touches **8)**Lateral Leg Swings **9)**Anterior/Posterior Leg Swings **10)**Calf Raises/Stretches

Workout: Perform 3 Circuits of the exercises at 50% of 1RM

Exercises	**Repetitions**
1. Squats	____/10-15 reps
2. Barbell Bench Press	____/10-15 reps
3. Incline Sit-ups	____/10-15 reps
4. Hyperextensions	____/10-15 reps
5. Upright Rows	____/10-15 reps
6. Hamstring Curls	____/10-15 reps
7. Lat Pull-downs	____/10-15 reps
8. Narrow Position Push-ups	____/10-15 reps
9. Dumbbell Shoulder Press	____/10-15 reps
10. Calf Raises	____/10-15 reps

Conditioning:

Aerobic Conditioning-	**Treadmill 10MW/5MR x 2**
Micro-Stretching	**Hold each stretch 40-60 Secs.**

Sample FAB Fitness weekly workout—Wednesday

Phase I—Anatomical Adaptation

Warm-up	Week-1
Stationary Bike/Elliptical	5-minutes
Dynamic Stretch	10X's Each Movement

1)Neck Rotations, **2)**Arm Rotations, **3)**Trunk Rotations **4)**Knee Rotations **5)**Ankle Rotations **6)**Walking High Knees **7)**Walking Toe Touches **8)**Lateral Leg Swings **9)**Anterior/Posterior Leg Swings **10)**Calf Raises/Stretches

Workout: Perform 3-Circuits of the exercises with bodyweight or dumbbells where possible. You have 30-secs. of work and 30 secs. To get to the next station and begin. You have 2-mins. Rest at the completion of a cycle.

Exercises	Repetitions*
1. Burpees	30 seconds
2. Tricep Press-ups	30 seconds
3. Standing Lunges	30 seconds
4. Standing Core Twists	30 seconds
5. Push-ups	30 seconds
6. Swiss Ball Crunches	30 seconds
7. Hitman	30 seconds
8. Weighted Cross Walks	30 seconds
9. Inch Worms	30 seconds
10. Lateral Lunges	30 seconds

Conditioning:

Anaerobic Conditioning-	6 x 40yds. Striders
	(30—Seconds rest in between each)
Micro-Stretching	**Hold each stretch for 40-60 Secs.**

Sample FAB Fitness weekly workout—Friday

*Each exercise is done for the maximum repetitions possible at your own pace during the time designated.

Phase I—Anatomical Adaptation

Warm-up	**Week-1**
Stationary Bike/Elliptical	5-minutes
Dynamic Stretch	10X's Each Movement

1)Neck Rotations, **2)**Arm Rotations, **3)**Trunk Rotations **4)**Knee Rotations **5)**Ankle Rotations **6)**Walking High Knees **7)**Walking Toe Touches **8)**Lateral Leg Swings **9)**Anterior/Posterior Leg Swings **10)**Calf Raises/Stretches

Workout: Perform 3-Circuits of the exercises with bodyweight or dumbbells where possible. You have 30-secs. of work and 30 secs. To get to the next station and begin. You have 2-mins. Rest at the completion of a cycle.

Exercises	**Repetitions***
1. Burpees	30 seconds
2. Tricep Press-ups	30 seconds
3. Standing Lunges	30 seconds
4. Standing Core Twists	30 seconds
5. Push-ups	30 seconds
6. Mountain Climbers	30 seconds
7. The Hitman	30 seconds
Guns Loader Series: **8.**Pummels, **9.**Upper Cuts, **10.**Curls	30 seconds each

Conditioning:

Anaerobic Conditioning-	**10X's Block Intervals** (Jog/Run your block, then walk back to the beginning)
Micro-Stretching	**Hold each stretch for 40-60 Secs.**

Sample Modified FAB Fitness Weekly Workout—Monday

*Each exercise is done for the maximum repetitions possible at your own pace during the time designated.

Phase I—Anatomical Adaptation

Warm-up	**Week-1**
Jogging in Place, Jumping Jacks, Way Backs	1-minute each movement
Dynamic Stretch	10X's Each Movement

1)Neck Rotations, **2)**Arm Rotations, **3)**Trunk Rotations **4)**Knee Rotations **5)**Ankle Rotations **6)**Walking High Knees **7)**Walking Toe Touches **8)**Lateral Leg Swings **9)**Anterior/Posterior Leg Swings **10)**Calf Raises/Stretches

Workout: Perform 3-Circuits of the exercises with bodyweight or dumbbells where possible. You have 30-secs. of work and 30 secs. to rest before beginning the next exercise. You have 2-mins. Rest at the completion of a cycle.

Exercises	**Repetitions***
1. Jump Squats	30 seconds
2. Tricep Press-ups	30 seconds
3. Standing Backwards Lunges	30 seconds
4. Rotating V-ups	30 seconds
5. Push-ups	30 seconds
6. Swiss Ball Crunches	30 seconds
7. Hitman	30 seconds
8. Double arm tricep-press	30 seconds
9. Inch Worms	30 seconds
10. Lateral Lunges	30 seconds

Conditioning:

Anaerobic Conditioning-	6 x 40yds. Striders
	(30—Seconds rest in between each)
Micro-Stretching	Hold each stretch for 40-60 Secs.

Sample Modified FAB Fitness Weekly Workout—Wednesday

*Each exercise is done for the maximum repetitions possible at your own pace during the time designated.

Chapter 31

UPLIFT
LEGACIES
R.E.A.P. what you S.O.E.™

Fiscal Fitness

Common catalysts for emotional upset within families and individuals are money problems. Sometimes the problems are unavoidable. As is the case of the current economy; evidenced by the collapse of the real estate market, and banking industry. Many people (including me) lost a lot of money investing in real estate when the housing bubble burst. Additionally, the unemployment and underemployment rates rose exponentially. These all contribute to our $14+ Trillion national debt that has continued to increase an average of $4.11 billion per day since September 28, 2007. I share these figures not as justifications, but for perspective. Because, even within this turmoil there are still very controllable aspects of our finances that will help us stay balanced and fiscally fit.

We each have choices to make relative to the stewardship of whatever resources we own and/or income we make. These choices will be indicative of the value system we're nurturing within our respective homes. A correctly aligned value system should also be executed. In other words, referencing the order of our individual PATS, we should never compromise a higher priority inspiration for one below it. This is how we effectively "Live our Creeds." Living a lifestyle beyond that which we can afford is likely to compromise our PATS order. Compounding debt with its impending stress and emotional upset will cause our lives to get out of balance. This is particularly evident in troubling economic times. We end up reactively seeking finances just to stay afloat, instead of proactively cultivating our objectives to get ahead.

The practiced idiom of "keeping up with the Joneses" has been the primary mechanism for many of the problems. The biblical reference is known as the tenth of the Ten Commandments, and is found in Exodus 20:17 "*You shall not covet your neighbor's house. You shall not covet your neighbor's wife, or his manservant or maidservant, his ox or donkey, or anything that belongs to your neighbor.*" Using the possessions of others as a measuring stick for our success is as irrational as assuming every man should be able to run 100 meters in 9.58 seconds because Usain Bolt (the World Record Holder) can.

"When we spend beyond our afforded lifestyle, we introduce unnecessary troubles."

We are each equipped with our own talents, skills, and passions. Ideally these should align with an appropriate purpose for our lives. From this purpose we are able to choose a career. Our careers will have varying degrees of incomes, which consequently provide relative lifestyles. When we spend beyond our afforded lifestyle, we introduce unnecessary troubles. Often times we're spending money we don't have, on things we don't need, to impress people we don't know (or at least with whom we don't have a relevant connection)! We end up setting ourselves up for self-inflicted struggles with conspicuous consumption. The fact is those who genuinely care for us don't care about our material possessions. They care about us. Even if we engage in self-serving consumption, or for benefit of our inner circle, affordability is still the number one consideration to preserve peace of mind.

"The fact is those who genuinely care for us don't care about our material possessions. They care about us."

People often mislabel material possessions and wealth as "Blessings." These are actually resources that can be used many ways (good and bad). Blessings therefore, are not associated with money or material things, but the fruit that sprout from how we utilize them. These fruit are noted in Galatians 5:22-23 "But the fruit of the Spirit is love, joy, peace, patience, kindness, goodness, faithfulness, gentleness, and self-control . . ." These are holistically characteristic of a sound spiritual life. They are not pick and choose virtues. That's what makes it most important that we not inject unnecessary pressures on our emotional health with the undue stress of living outside our means. Of course this, like many other ideals, is easier said in theory than practiced experientially. Believe me, I know. Planning is still the key.

"But the fruit of the Spirit is love, joy, peace, patience, kindness, goodness, faithfulness, gentleness, and self-control . . ."
-Galatians 5: 22-23

Holding ourselves tangibly responsible for "Living our Creeds" by living within our means is our most practical tool to succeed. Many have heard the misused pretext "Money is the root of all evil!" This is a misquoted and untrue statement. The actual quote is from 1 Timothy 6:10 and is "For the LOVE of money is a root of all sorts of evil, and some by longing for it have wandered away from the faith and pierced themselves with many griefs." Money is not the problem. It's our attitude towards it. We are to love people, not money or things. Unfortunately, the materialistic and capitalistic society in which we live causes even those of the purest intent to go astray. Most people within my inner circle are familiar with the phrase "like it a lot." It's my immediately response anytime anyone says that they love anything other than an entity of their faith, or a person. This is another of my intentional paradigm shifts from the norm. We should utilize the power of love in its proper context. Nothing temporal and material should be loved. Though, we can certainly "like it a lot."

We make value statements via expenditure of our time, talents, and treasures. Plans are pertinent to proper allocation of our treasures, just as with time and talents. Accountability within each is best gauged by a quantifiable and tangible medium. There are many approaches to allocating our assets responsibly. Those with proper knowledge and self-discipline might effectively formulate their own plans. Historically, that has not been the case for most people. My suggestion is to sit down with an Insurance and Financial Services Professional to go over strategies that might best fit your objectives.

After many years of trial and error, I had to incorporate a tangible plan in my own life to keep my material "treasures" on track. I call it a *Proactive Asset Allocation Manager*^{TM} (PA^{2}M). Each of the strategies is derived from monthly income. Our lifestyles should be designed around an appropriate percentage of this amount. The idea is to provide a balanced distribution between current spending, short/intermediate term plans, and long term plans.

Each of us has a predetermined tax bracket by income and marital status. The primary individual variable for net income is itemized deductions. So our spendable income will vary accordingly. But there are general considerations that we all should weigh. The first are pre-tax income deductions. I've found it pertinent to take advantage of pre-tax income deductions, like employer-sponsored health insurance, and other benefits. Having experienced the exorbitant costs and limitations of independent health care, I've found no better value than comprehensive coverage subsidized by employers. When I became a company owner, it was still a better value to put together a benefits package including health coverage for full time employees than to purchase individual health policies for my family.

Next, I allocate savings to my employers' 401(K) plans that at least maximize the matching contributions from the companies. I've had companies match anywhere from one-half to double the employee contributions. Regardless of market conditions, with a guaranteed 50% to 200% return, those are great financial vehicles to subsidize intermediate and long term plans. There are various other options in this area depending on the type of company, including 403b's for Non-profits, and 457 plans for some government entities. However, since these employer-qualified retirement plans are limited, I've never relied on them solely.

The Out of sight, Out of mind Principle: "It's much easier to stay within a monthly budget when the only funds available to us with ease of liquidity are those making up the monthly budgeted figure."

The next two allocations are simultaneously made to both my current spending (everyday transactions) and short/intermediate (up to 15 years) planning accounts. The comfort number I settled on for a maximum monthly budget is 60% of gross household income. This is the area of current spending, and requires the most discipline. We have to decide that we are willing to live within our means at a level that allows for additional allocation of our monthly income. The most practical way I've found to institute this discipline is to deposit only the 60% amount in my checking account on a monthly basis. It's the "Out of sight, Out of mind" Principle. It's much easier to stay within a monthly budget when the only funds available to us with ease of liquidity are those making up the monthly budgeted figure. If we deposit our entire income in readily accessible accounts on a monthly basis then we're more likely to use all of the funds in the accounts. Conversely, we won't consider "out of sight" funds as available.

A sustainable lifestyle has to take into account the uncertainties of life. Included are possible periods of unemployment, unforeseen large medical expenses, temporary or permanent disabilities, or premature deaths. The funds utilized to meet these unfortunate occurrences are accumulated in short/intermediate planning. Emergency Reserves should be accumulated as quickly as possible. A nice starting guideline is 3-6 months of the household's monthly budget. The shorter timeframe would be attributable to those people more established in their careers, or with lower liabilities. Additional considerations for short and intermediate plans are savings for things like starting a business or paying down on a new home.

"Nearly half of all mortgage foreclosures are due to disability."

A sound plan also incorporates both disability and life insurance for the income earning adults, and at least life insurance for the remaining household members. Nearly half of all mortgage foreclosures are due to disability. Statistically, nearly one-third of Americans entering the work force today (3 in 10) will become disabled before they retire. Within the Social Security Administration January 2009 Fact Sheet, 18% of the population classified themselves as either fully or partially disabled. It's a great idea to take advantage of this benefit through the subsidized offerings of most corporate employers. If this is not available find out what options exist through an Insurance and Financial Services Professional. Insuring our income (even if just a percentage of it) is crucial to guarding against the unexpected set-backs we might face. Disability is one that occurs more often than most people are aware.

Life insurance is a very touchy and personal subject. It gets even touchier when referencing our children. Not very many people enjoy talking about the possibility of dying. However, pretending that it will never happen is not very responsible. Nor will it keep us from dying someday anyway. The average life expectancy in the US as of March, 2011 was 78.1 years. Also, out of 100,000 people born in a given year, 83,057 (or 83.057%) should still be alive at age 65. Only 2,523 (or 2.523%) will be alive at age 100. An identifiable birth date is common to all included within these statistics; whereas the death dates exist in the unknown of all except the dead. Therefore, it makes sense to have a plan in place to attend to our commitments and responsibilities regardless of when our date becomes certain. Particularly significant are the other people dependent upon us financially.

I talk with a number of people (usually young) who feel they don't need life insurance at this stage of their lives because they are without dependents, and don't carry any debt that would be a detriment to anyone else. There are even those who profess that they will continue in such an independent and single state for the remainder of their lives. If you can relate to their position, then the following retort is fitting for you as well. Besides people who are unfortunately uninsurable and individuals with the great fortune of being self-insured, everybody else would be well served to invest in life insurance.

Change is certain to occur throughout the lives of those people blessed to meet or exceed the 78.1 years of life expectancy. One of those changes is our health. Great health today does not guarantee great health tomorrow. So, one advantage for any healthy person getting life insurance is that it locks in their insurability should an unforeseen circumstance occur that changes their health in the future. The other change that occurs is the carefree single no-dependents young adult of yesterday oftentimes becomes the wiser married-with-kids mature adult of tomorrow. Whereas the younger version thought s/he didn't need life insurance at all, the older self wishes s/he would have gotten it way back then when it was more affordable.

On the concept of self-insurability, I have the following simple strategy based on the aforementioned life expectancy: Without earning anymore income, if a person doesn't have the liquid resources (or those in easily liquidated form) to provide for themselves through their life expectancy, provide for their dependents throughout their dependency, and provide for a dependent spouse for his/her respective life expectancy then s/he is NOT self-insured. The people with such resources are few and far between. That's why life insurance is the best way to bridge the financial gap and create legacies for the masses.

In the case of children, the purchase of life insurance on them accomplishes two things: (1) It insures their insurability by covering them at their youngest and healthiest; and (2) It allows the parents who love them the time to grieve should such a family tragedy occur. As a parent of three children for whom I would give my own life, I know if I lost either of them I would certainly need grieving time. Business as usual would have to wait. Fact is, life insurance allows the hopes and dreams of loved ones to continue on if the unforeseen premature death occurs for any family members.

Historically, the legacy of middle to lower income Americans has not been to leave financial assets to loved ones, but liabilities. It's been a recycled habit of primarily living check to check. At the death of one generation the final expenses and debts are usually passed to the next, and the cycle repeats. For pennies on the dollar life insurance provides a means to help establish new Legacies even if our life's journey is cut short.

"Historically, the legacy of middle to lower income Americans has not been to leave financial assets to loved ones, but liabilities."

Many people are concerned with cost, while others are stifled trying to determine the kind or amount to purchase. If a successful life of excellence is the objective, then these obstacles must be quickly overcome by budgetary prioritization. Ignorance in any area is bliss only until the point when we are enlightened. As it relates to caring for those whom we profess love, how we distribute our resources speaks profoundly to our expression of it. Regardless of financial constraints, life insurance is not an option of sound prioritized family spending. We make value statements in how we spend our money.

Most insurable individuals can find some form of life insurance for a relatively small monthly payment when compared to the death benefit. So we must make sure we express a value in those we love by fitting their well-being within our budgets. As far as type of insurance, the best kind of life insurance to purchase is whatever kind an individual can afford to have in force at the time of his/her death. Surviving family members will not be concerned with the type of insurance that delivered the death benefits. It's the fact that we cared enough to provide for their delivery. Some people get so caught up in the intricacies of the options that they never choose one.

" . . . the best kind of life insurance to purchase is whatever kind an individual can afford to have in force at the time of his/her death."

Only 61% of adult Americans have any life insurance protection at all. Unfortunately, even in those cases most are underinsured. According to statistics from industry research and consulting firm LIMRA International, the average American household carries just $126,000 in life insurance—approximately $300,000 less than they actually need.

There are quantitative methods of calculating the correct amount. The two I've found most helpful are Perpetual Income Replacement (*PIR*) and the comprehensive LIFE needs analysis. For the majority of people their most valuable asset is their ability to earn an income. Therefore, insuring it is the most responsible financial strategy available. With *PIR*, we can calculate the amount of annual income needed by a family indefinitely, and divide it by the decimal percentage of a conservative rate of return (i.e. $50,000 income divided by .05 or 5% APR equals a $1,000,000 life insurance need). This scenario would provide an indefinite annual income of $50,000 for the family from a $1,000,000 death benefit fully invested and earning 5% annual returns. The figure should be estimated by each of us individually relative to our own suitability, risk tolerance, and the type of account in which the money will be deposited.

"For most people their most valuable asset is their ability to earn an income."

With the comprehensive approach, we take the letters of the acronym LIFE and calculate the need based upon the relative meaning of each as follows:

L—Represents Loans or any form of outstanding debt.

I—Represents the amount of Income we wish to provide for the family whether for a certain period of time or indefinitely.

F—Represents Final expenses in the form of burial costs or final outstanding medical bills.

E—Represents either Educational costs for children or another adult. Additionally, it might represent an Endowment we may wish to leave heirs, an organization, or charitable cause for which we currently provide support.

With either method, any current resources that might assist the family are taken into consideration and subtracted from the calculated figure to get the final need amount. Most people who do either of these calculations are astonished by the large amount of the resulting figure. Awareness of the ideal objective is important to eventually get there, even if it's not possible within today's budget. The key is to at least have something, and for those who now know their real number it's likely that at least the $126,000 average will increase.

One of my family's personal tragedies inspires my passion for life insurance as a cornerstone feature of any sound financial structure. The loss in January, 1980 of the most accomplished member of our extended family caused us much emotional distress. However, because my aunt Bernice purchased life insurance, her loved ones didn't suffer financially as a result of her premature death. Bernice was my mother's oldest sister. She was very well educated with multiple degrees, including a Masters in Special Education. She was also very well respected as an educator, as a leader in the community, and by her family. Unfortunately, she was diagnosed with breast cancer at the age of 35 and lost her battle at the tender age of 38. Prior to her passing she asked my parents if they could assist her husband in caring for her two sons Reggie and Shannon. As was expected of the "Dynamic Two" they, with heavy but warm hearts, accepted the opportunity to assist a loved one with her dying wish. There were logistical matters to their acceptance that would cause many unprepared families problems carrying out the duties. The boys lived in Waco, Texas with their father, and we lived in Fort Valley, Georgia. Whether the boys came to live with us, or my parents took regular trips to Texas, there would certainly be an expense to this "assistance." With already limited resources and four children of their own, my parents would be stretching finances to the limits. Thankfully though, Bernice had already taken into consideration the financial well being of her sons with life insurance administered through a trust for them. This allowed my parents to assist as they would have regardless, but without causing additional financial stress on our nuclear family. This scenario could have very easily gone the other way without proper planning by my aunt Bernice.

As is evident by the extent to which I covered the topic, life insurance is the only entity of a sound financial plan applicable to all three phases. Whether considering current spending ability, short/intermediate plans, or long term plans, the premature death of a family member can put an immediate halt to many hopes and dreams. Life insurance serves as a tool to assist us with keeping those objectives alive during any phase of our plan should the unforeseen occur.

The last phase of a sound financial plan is the Long Term. This is where we provide for long range objectives (20+ years away) like children's college funds, financial independence (commonly referenced as retirement), or bequests. These long range objectives should only be funded after a proper emergency fund, disability insurance, and life insurance are in place. Each unfortunate event funded by these tools would otherwise drain any long term accounts anyway. However, if the short/intermediate term accounts and insurance needs are met then long term planning is viable.

College funds should be simply based on what you would like to provide as a dollar amount to help fund your children's post-secondary education. Consideration should also be made if you would like to help fund any graduate or doctoral programs. There are a number of options to look into whether through individual savings, tax-advantaged 529 plans, or State-sponsored prepaid tuition plans. Either way, consistent savings over a number of years are much more affordable than taking on the impending costly college tuition bill all at once.

Most of us look forward to a day in the future when it is no longer necessary to work for a living. This period of our lives is commonly referenced as retirement. However, following the theme of finding a career within our passions, I've labeled this objective Financial Independence. The idea is to plan for a point in our lives when we will no longer need to earn a paycheck for a living, but can utilize our time and talents however we choose. For some that may be continuing in our careers, doing charitable work, or traveling. Regardless, we'll have the option to do that which we desire most while living, rather than what we must just to stay alive.

Bequests or endowments are the part of our financial plan that either establish or sustain our legacy. These may be provided for children or other relatives and friends. Some may also want to leave financial support for an organization (like a church) or charitable cause (like the American Cancer Society). As previously shared, even if our incomes are unable to provide for such an accumulated savings, life insurance is a great source for creating an instant legacy.

On the following page I've shared a visual illustration of my Proactive Asset Allocation Manager. Included are also example accounts for funding the various phases. As previously shared, I highly suggest sitting down with an Insurance and Financial Services Professional to help structure a personal financial plan for you and your family. Be sure to make a plan based on your own risk tolerance and product suitability. In other words, make sure you are the benefactor considered in the strategies of your plan, not your adviser. As is the case for all objectives of a successful life, not all plans are the same. But the key is to actually have one.

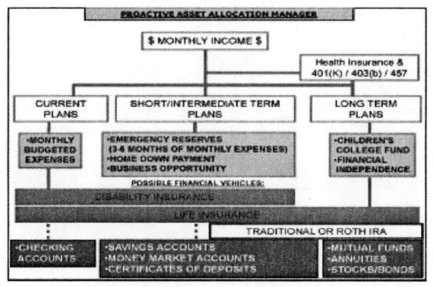

My Cash Management System

Chapter 32

 he Success Playbook

"Life is not lived in Procedures, but in Processes."

There are five elements to attaining our success: (1) Desire, (2) Planning, (3) Preparation, (4) Execution, and (5) Accomplishment. Through the systems within this book, you can bring each to fruition. As a former professional football player I was blessed over the years with exposure to many structured approaches to development, coaching, and execution of the tasks of my sport. There were certainly some variations between different teams on many different levels during my 25 years of organized participation in football. However, what was consistently present at all levels was a tangible strategy. The strategies always focused on meeting team objectives. The team objectives were met through coordinating properly executed individual assignments of the players. These assigned plans were our playbooks.

After a number of years of studying, practicing, and executing these tasks it would seem that we would grasp strategies and plays to the degree that the playbooks would become obsolete. However, there are two problems with this idea: (1) The sport continued to evolve with new strategies introduced as fast as we could grasp them; and (2) We didn't get to play the same team every week. Therefore, just like the strategies, the playbooks were ever-evolving resources. Additionally, in order to meet the specific demands associated with preparing to play a different team each week we had to create customized executable game plans from the plethora of strategies within our playbooks. This was a consistent process throughout my football career. Pop Warner champions and NFL Super Bowl champions use the same platform: Create a strategic plan based on a proven philosophy for sustainable success and pick the appropriate players to execute it. The principles and strategies shared within this book are designed to become playbooks for life. These can then be personalized and strategically organized into our own game plans.

In order to begin writing your game plan, first prioritize your inspirations. The order is completely up to you. But you won't persistently work any plan without important motivators to get through tough times. Recall your Proactive Attributions To Success. And begin your plan with them to inspire the journey.

After you've defined the "why you do", move on to the "what you do". This involves evaluating your strengths and weaknesses. We must know our unique potential to be a success in order to reach it. Therefore, in general, we're not seeking what is outside of the skills with which we've been blessed. A successful life involves an excellent plan geared toward individual potential. There are multiple areas to analyze: physical talents, intellectual retention, communication skills, etc. Ideally you would like to find a path associated with your biggest strength. However, you also want to evaluate your level of passion for the activity. If you don't have a passion for what you are doing, then whether or not you're great at performing it has little meaning. The most sustainable path to greatness will have both proficiency for and a fondness of performing relevant activities.

Chapter 33

The +One Principle™

Once we've addressed our inspirations and relevant abilities, it's time to draw from this Playbook of principles those strategies that are appropriate and relative to our life objectives. Make them specific and measureable. Quantifiable objectives are important pieces of a successful life. Be deliberate in gauging your progress. Is it what you wanted? If so, keep it up . . . If not, make adjustments. If you keep doing what you've always done, you'll keep getting what you've always gotten.

I recall my light bulb moment to this concept. One day during football practice my high school position coach, Ed Mullins caught a couple of my teammates and me singing and dancing on the sideline. He pulled me aside and proceeded with quite the admonishing. However, in the midst of it, he taught me a great lesson. He shared that he saw something special in me, and that I would have some opportunities to do some great things. His caveat was that I needed to understand I can't get caught up just doing the same things as everybody else. He told me to have fun, but treat this like it is serious business and I'll become one of the best football players around. During that exchange Coach Mullins also became the first person—outside of my family and close friends—who told me he thought I could play in the National Football League someday.

From that day forward I instituted my *⁺One Principle*™ (Plus One). Besides no longer goofing off in practice, I challenged myself to always do more than what was asked or expected of me. Whenever we'd run sprints after practice, I would always do at least one more than we were asked to do. As the years went on throughout college and into the pros, every now and then I'd get a teammate or two to join me. This concept has also been transferable to my personal and professional life outside of sports. It will work for you as well. Just be cognizant of the fact the same old normal and usual activities do not equate to excellent input. So we can't expect excellent output from them. As Bishop Dale C. Bronner once shared, "You cannot do ordinary things and expect extraordinary results. Our goal is to make extraordinary our norm.

"You cannot do ordinary things and expect extraordinary results."
-Dale C. Bronner

The paradigm shift of this playbook for life starts with its strategic name: *Conditioning 4 Excellence* requires that we open our minds to a higher level of living. The use of the word "conditioning" suggests a challenging, systematic series of activities designed to produce the best you possible in mind, body, and spirit. The value is to be evident professionally and personally, within vital activities to mundane tasks. Additionally, it denotes a perpetual process never to be deemed complete until our life is over. To be our best, we will need very similar approaches to those that elite performers use to become professional baseball's World Series winners, basketball's NBA Finals victors, and football's Super Bowl champions. Our use of strategic playbooks and executable game plans for success in life will likewise involve challenging lengthy processes—not simple instantaneous procedures.

"True SUCCESS will never be measured in $Dollars$, but in SENSE: Common SENSE to discern a SENSE of clarity, focus, passion, joy, contentment, and commitment in our journeys. All are critical to our best SENSE of self!"

Today's society is infatuated with instant gratification. However, life is not lived in procedures but in processes. That which is nurtured over time develops deeper roots, which allows us to weather storms. So for even the best laid strategies and plans to materialize we must exercise patience. And patience is unfortunately an uncommon virtue. Instead of prudently evaluating themselves, vetting their relationships, and setting on a relative life path, many pick the first thing that looks promising. This often leads to poor career choices and discontent. Our evaluations of who we are and what we are going to become should involve far more than a quick glance. We must commit to honest self-observation and evaluation of our strengths and weaknesses in order to choose relevant activities and formulate applicable objectives. Many also fail to consider whether or not they have a genuine passion for what they choose to do. True success will never be a third-party measure of dollars, but a firsthand acquisition of sense: common sense to discern a sense of clarity, focus, passion, joy, contentment, and commitment in our individual journeys. All are critical to a best sense of self! The process isn't instantaneous; it can take a lifetime.

I challenge you to UPLIFT your mind today. Stop using the word "good" and start referencing "great;" stop being "okay" and start feeling "excellent;" discontinue the "pursuit of happiness" and cultivate a "state of joy." Think of how often we say or hear "good morning", "good day", or "good night". Who was so conditioned in mediocrity that s/he coined these universally accepted salutations? Is adequate really our ultimate desire? I'm certain that's not the case for those reading this book! So please, when we meet, offer up a wish for a "great morning", "great day" or "great night" and I'll be sure to reciprocate the same. Excellence doesn't tolerate mediocrity. Make your own decision to be excellent today.

"A successful life is defined not at its end, but in the contentment enjoyed by its host while living!"

Are you in positive foundational relationships? Have you discovered and aligned your inspirations and talents? Do you have a core belief system that instructs you to do what's right? Are you systematically developing your natural gifts? Have you defined success? Do you have a plan to reach it? Your journey will be fueled by your attitude. Be positive, persistent, and passionate! These are all things over which you have control. Then, when it's evaluation time the only opinion that matters will be your own. The choice is yours: let us not confuse being alive with living! We get but one mortal life. Our inspirations and decisions determine our enjoyment during it and our eternal resting place after it.

No one gets to define success for us. Nor do they decide whether or not we feel accomplished spiritually, personally, intellectually, or professionally? They can't because success is not an objectively quantifiable term. Think about how we could go about measuring it? No one can for someone else, because it's relative. If we let other people decide whether or not what we are doing with our life is successful; we will be on a constant roller-coaster of accomplishments and failures, chasing someone else's dreams. Whether or not an individual has achieved success is based on the individual. Our own inspirations should reveal our aspirations. And strategic cultivation of talents and skills will help get us there.

For me success is "lifting as I climb." On my life's resume I have college degrees, an NFL career, and successful businesses. I have almost every academic honor that there was to earn, and more designations, certifications, and awards than most. However, those ancillary things will mean nothing at the end of my life. Not a single person will be UPLIFTed by a piece of paper stating what I accomplished in the classroom or in business, how well I played football, or how intelligent I was. They'll be impacted by the difference made in their lives by getting out into their world and doing something to help make things better. This has not to this point happened by chance, nor will it ever. It takes an intentional effort.

We often hear salutations of "good luck" when starting a new challenge. That's another word usage I did away with long ago. To me there is no such thing as luck. There are certainly varying degrees of opportunities—both good and bad. However, regardless of when and how opportunities present themselves, we must be prepared to take advantage of them. As has been evident to me in my life, Roman 8:28 applies to both presumably good and bad experiences. Luck infers that life is a series of coincidental meetings with positive and negative fortune. We have ordered steps to personal prosperity if we just follow the predesigned path by a Divine Designer.

When your name is called, are you ready for "Showtime?" Are you Conditioning 4 Excellence while living your dreams? A successful life is defined not at its end, but in the contentment enjoyed by its host while living! Prioritize, organize, and make your dreams materialize. Use this playbook to create and execute your game plan. Fortunate is he who is ready when his opportunities arrive, because luck has nothing to do with it. Your success is in YOU . . . LET'S GET IT!

FROM MY HEART, THROUGH THESE WORDS, IS HIS MESSAGE!

$\mathscr{B}$OOKS WORTH READING:

- The Glorious Journey by Charles Stanley
- A Leader in the Making by Joyce Meyer
- The Five Love Languages by Gary Chapman
- The Secret of Loving by Josh McDowell
- The 360 Degree Leader by John C. Maxwell
- The Purpose Driven Life by Rick Warren
- If You Want to Walk on Water, You've Got to Get Out of the Boat by John Ortberg
- The Act of Marriage by Tim & Beverly LaHaye
- Before You Do by T.D. Jakes
- If Only He Knew by Gary Smalley
- Relationship Rescue by Phillip C. McGraw, PH.D.
- Quiet Strength by Tony Dungy
- The Energy Bus by Jon Gordon
- All Buts Stink! by Walter Bond
- Self Matters by Phillip C. McGraw, PH.D.
- The Love Dare by Stephen & Alex Kendrick
- His Needs Her Needs by Williard F. Harley, Jr.
- The One by Williard F. Harley, Jr.
- The Original biblical Manuscripts by GOD through 40 inspired men.

𝒲ISDOM LIFE REVEALS:

1. Life reveals . . . that we must first clearly identify our inspirations in order to achieve our aspirations.
2. Life reveals . . . that character is built in our nurturing, but manifests itself in our trials.
3. Life reveals . . . that success always has company, but failure seems to travel alone.
4. Life reveals . . . that Jesus does not care what man thinks of me.
5. Life reveals . . . that the love we parents have for our children is the best human example we'll ever have of agape (unconditional) love.
6. Life reveals . . . that customers are loyal to good prices and clients are loyal to good people.
7. Life reveals . . . that it is important to live mindful of the legacy we leave behind, for our deeds are not undone in our passing.
8. Life reveals . . . when establishing new relationships, we initially meet the personality . . . but in time we will get to know the character.
9. Life reveals . . . that people of excellence endure disappointment without loss of enthusiasm.
10. Life reveals . . . that coincidence is God's way of remaining anonymous.
11. Life reveals . . . that it doesn't matter if you have the skill for a task if you don't have the will to effectively get it done.
12. Life reveals . . . that God allows dismay not to scare us to death, but to inspire us to life.
13. Life reveals . . . that death does not care how much you earn, but life does.
14. Life reveals . . . that it's vital to feel great about who I am, because I'm preparing for who I'll be.
15. Life reveals . . . that it's alright to delegate some of my activities, but never my responsibilities.
16. Life reveals . . . that excellence is revealed in the effort, and not necessarily in the attainment.
17. Life reveals . . . that the excellent way is the only way to succeed.
18. Life reveals . . . that it's necessary to plan, prepare, and execute (not just wish and dream) for success.

19. Life reveals . . . that we must cultivate our crafts, while carefully discerning our pursuits.
20. Life reveals . . . that my value is not about me, but He who dwells in me makes me priceless!
21. Life reveals . . . that the fruit of Joy is not subject to our circumstances.
22. Life reveals . . . that a positive attitude is a catalyst to exceptional achievements.
23. Life reveals . . . that it's important to not let circumstances affect my attitude—but instead, to let my attitude affect my circumstances.
24. Life reveals . . . that a woman's need for emotional contentment outweighs her need for practical fulfillment.
25. Life reveals . . . that I need to be selective in my choice of friends, for they will both influence me, and be my best reflection.
26. Life reveals . . . that we should always be lifting as we climb.
27. Life reveals . . . that our best testimony is found in our actions, and that we should use words only when necessary.
28. Life reveals . . . that love is a verb.
29. Life reveals . . . that the world is in dire need of UPLIFT (United People Living In Foundational Truth).
30. Life reveals . . . that there is no firmer foundation than that found in a relationship with Jesus Christ.
31. Life reveals . . . that there is only one race populating our world: the human race.
32. Life reveals . . . that letting go and "letting God" works.
33. Life reveals . . . that it's better to cultivate the way to an objective than to just stumble upon one.

ℒIBRARY OF UPLIFT APTITUDES:

- Ability—capability to perform
- Acceptance—understanding or respecting the virtues of an idea
- Accountability—willingness to accept responsibility for one's actions and promises.
- Adaptability—versatility and flexibility to change when needed.
- Altruism—demonstrating a selfless concern for others.
- Aspiration—a goal or ambition
- Assertiveness—aggressiveness; ability to voice one's position comfortably
- Autonomy—independence; independent behavior; self-governed
- Awareness—present knowledge of
- Balance—weighted evenly
- Benevolence—goodwill, desire to do good
- Candor—honesty; sincerity; frankness
- Caring—a sincere feeling of concern
- Caution—an alertness in a dangerous situation; to warn
- Charity—cheerful giving
- Chastity—prudent behavior
- Citizenship—actively involved in the betterment of one's community, state, and country.
- Cleanliness—maintaining a clean person and environment
- Commitment—explicit dedication
- Compassion—heartfelt understanding of someone or something
- Communication—focus on understanding and being understood.
- Confidence—self-assurance
- Conscientiousness—keen, particular awareness
- Consideration—thoughtfulness of others
- Contentment—having a feeling of fulfillment
- Cooperativeness—working along with
- Courage—willingness to state one's beliefs and/or to take personal risks to achieve goals or objectives.
- Creativity—ability to generate new ideas in thinking or vision; originality

- Cunning—craftiness; skill demonstrated in a slick manner
- Curiosity—the desire to know or learn more
- Dependability—trustworthiness
- Determination—commitment to a goal
- Discernment—ability to draw clear meaning from that which is obscure
- Empathy—ability to show concern by vicariously experiencing a situation through the feeling, thought, and attitudes of another individual.
- Encouragement—motivational support
- Enthusiasm—demonstrated excitement
- Equanimity—calmness, particularly under pressure; balance
- Fairness—just treatment
- Faithfulness—fidelity within a relationship
- Foresight—consideration before an action occurs
- Forgiveness—the release of bad feeling or grudges against another for his/her actions
- Fortitude—strength, particularly when facing challenges
- Friendliness—expressive kindness
- Generosity—readiness in giving or sharing
- Gentleness—careful treatment or handling
- Goodness—without negative thought or intent; positivity
- Gratitude—showing appreciation
- Helpfulness—willingness to assist others.
- Honesty—truth; truthful treatment
- Honor—upstanding character
- Hopefulness—attitude of positive thoughts
- Hospitality—kind and generous treatment of others
- Humility—acknowledging one's gifts are not to be taken for granted; recognizing personal role in accomplishments is but one part of a collaboration of talented and skilled individuals.
- Humor—a comic quality causing amusement; the trait of understanding what is amusing
- Impartiality—objectivity; ability to take a fair, neutral position with opposing ideas
- Independence—self sufficiency
- Individualism—confidence in one's uniqueness, independent thought or actions

- Ingenuity—cleverness; the quality of being inventive or finding a way to succeed in difficult times or when facing a challenge
- Initiative—recognizing that actions need to be taken and being proactive with little or no supervision.
- Integrity—having a moral code to do good through ethical and honest behavior.
- Intelligence—capacity for learning and understanding; aptitude in grasping truths, meanings, relationships and such
- Intuition—the perception of truth, fact or action without reason
- Inventiveness—industriousness fueled by creativity
- Joy—exceptional delight or contentment regardless of external circumstances
- Justice—fair treatment
- Kindness—expressed concern/care for others
- Knowledge—accumulation of information, facts, truths
- Leadership—makes development of others a top priority by setting clear expectations, providing on-going feedback, coaching/ training, and mentoring (by personal example).
- Logic—evidenced by rational decisions.
- Lovingness—expressively displaying love or affection
- Loyalty—commitment; dedicated support
- Meekness—gentleness; kindness; humble patience
- Mercy—compassionate favor shown toward an offender or someone undeserving
- Moderation—without excess or extremes
- Modesty—unassuming of one's own skills or talents
- Morality—conformity to values or rules of conduct; virtuous conduct
- Nobility—admirable behavior or distinguished character
- Nonviolence—action without physical altercation
- Nurturing—supportive and encouraging; nourishing
- Obedience—acceptance of the rules or laws
- Openness—honesty; candor; the willingness to share oneself
- Optimism—positive outlook
- Order—organization
- Passion—energetic, optimistic, and invigorates others with an internal drive for excellence. Demonstrating enthusiasm.
- Patience—understanding in extended times of challenge

- Peacefulness—calmness; contented spirit
- Perseverance—determination; the quality of never giving up
- Philomathy—having an affinity for learning and new ideas.
- Piety—reverence for God; devotion to religious practices
- Potential—a characteristic of promise in what is possible
- Poverty—the state of being without, particularly material items
- Prudence—conservative thinking; caution with regard to practical matters; discretion
- Purity—wholesomeness
- Purposefulness—having meaning; acting with deliberate intent
- Reason—rationality; organized, logical thinking
- Readiness—preparedness; the quality of being prepared for an opportunity
- Remembrance—a recall of the past; a tangible or intangible symbol of the past
- Resilience—the ability to bounce back after challenges
- Respectfulness—honor
- Responsibility—accountability; being relied upon for action
- Restraint—self-control, particularly in times of pressure or stress
- Reverence—Respect; extremely high regard
- Self-awareness—knowing one's own strengths and shortcomings.
- Self-confidence—a belief in one's ability to achieve.
- Self-discipline—self-control; the ability to stay focused on a goal, particularly in the presence of temptation
- Self-reliance—dependence on one's self
- Self-respect—honoring one's self, and particularly one's values
- Sensitivity—empathetic compassion; understanding and caring feeling of action for another
- Service—giving of one's time and effort
- Sharing—willingness to give of one's own resources to assist others.
- Sincerity—genuine feeling
- Spirituality—connectedness to a higher being or God
- Strength—internal resolution; the ability to endure
- Sympathy—ability to effectively demonstrate concern for others in times of sorrow, disappointment, or pain.
- Tactfulness—ability to behave and communicate in an appropriately empathetic manner.

- Talent—a special natural ability or aptitude; a predisposed superior quality capable of relative achievement or success.
- Teamwork—encourages collaboration to achieve collective goals or objectives.
- Temperance—ability to maintain self-control.
- Tenacity—ability to remain tough and resilient; and keep going even when conditions aren't favorable.
- Thankfulness—to show appreciation through words and actions.
- Thoughtfulness—kind consideration of others
- Trustworthiness—dependability; proving one can be depended on when consistently challenged
- Truthfulness—honesty; candor
- Understanding—acceptance of another or another's perspective
- Unity—togetherness
- Vision—the ability to clearly create, define, and communicate a plan towards a realistic and credible future
- Wisdom—experientially acquired knowledge/discernment; the ability to make right decisions

*W*ISDOM QUOTES:

Cowardice asks the question, "Is it safe?" Expedience asks the question, "Is it possible?" Vanity asks the question, "Is it popular?" But conscience asks the question, "Is it right?" . . . And there comes a time when one must take a position that is neither safe, nor politic, nor popular; but one must take it because one's conscience tells one that it is right!
-Dr. Martin Luther King, Jr.

To argue with a person who has renounced the use of reason is like administering medicine to the dead . . . .
-Thomas Paine

My fellow Americans; ask not what your country can do for you—ask what you can do for your country.
-John F. Kennedy

Honesty isn't the best policy—it is the only policy.
-George Mecherle

The quality of a man's life is in direct proportion to his commitment to excellence, regardless of his chosen field of endeavor.
-Vince Lombardi

Only those who dare to fail greatly can achieve greatly.
-Robert F. Kennedy

You can't build a reputation on what you're planning to do.
-Henry Ford

There is an island of opportunity in the middle of every difficulty.
-Anonymous

The opposite of faith is not doubt; it is certainty.
-Ann LaMott

Lifting as we climb
-Omega Psi Phi Fraternity Inc.

Our greatest glory is not in never falling, but in rising every time we fall.
-Confucius

Strong lives are motivated by dynamic purposes.
-Kenneth Hildebrand

Success seems to be largely a matter of hanging on after others have let go.
-Joseph Addison

Enthusiasm is the vital element toward the individual success of every man or woman.
-Conrad Hilton
The penalty of affluence is that it cuts one off from the common lot, common experience, and common fellowship.
-Arnold Toynbee

Show me a guy who's afraid to look bad, and I'll show you a guy you can beat every time.
-Lou Brock

The best things in life aren't things.
-Art Buchwald

Humility does not mean you think less of yourself. It means you think of yourself less.
-Ken Blanchard

The race is not always to the swift, but to those who keep on running.
-Anonymous

Right is right, even if everyone is against it; and wrong is wrong, even if everyone is for it.
-William Penn

True faith does not contradict its words by its conduct.
-Unknown

Love is a gift, not a reward for service.
-Jack Winter

The more I want to get something done, the less I call it work.
-*Richard Bach*

Inside the will of God there is no failure. Outside the will of God there is no success.
-*Bernard Edinger*

When in doubt, tell the truth.
-*Mark Twain*

If your ship doesn't come in, swim out to it.
-*Jonathan Winters*

Failure is a stepping-stone to greatness.
-*Oprah Winfrey*

The art of acceptance is the art of making someone who has just done you a small favor wish that he might have done you a greater one.
-*Russell Lynes*

Man can live for about forty days without food, and about three days without water, about eight minutes without air . . . but only for one second without hope.
-*Hal Lindsey*

Joy is not in things; it is in us.
-Richard Wagner

You never achieve real success unless you (have a passion for) what you are doing.
-Dale Carnegie

Be a life long or short, its completeness depends on what it was lived for.
-David Starr Jordan

Good, better, best: Never let it rest, until your good is better and your better is your best.
-Anonymous

A man cannot do good(things) before he is made good.
-Martin Luther

In order to attract more of the blessings that life has to offer, you must truly appreciate what you already have.
-Ralph Marston

Don't judge each day by the harvest you reap, but by the seeds you plant.
-Robert Louis Stevenson

Good works do not make a good man, but a good man does good works.
-Martin Luther

More people would learn from their mistakes if they weren't so busy denying them.
-Harold J. Smith

The quality of individuals is reflected in the standards that they set for themselves.
-Ray Kroc

It is never too late to be what you might have been.
-George Eliot

Destiny is no matter of chance. It is a matter of choice. It is not a thing to be waited for, it is a thing to be achieved.
-*William Jennings Bryan*

The measure of a life is not its duration, but its donation.
-*Corrie Ten Boom*

Work as if everything depended on you and pray as if everything depended on God.
-*D.L. Moody*

We get exactly the problems we need in our life to fix the things about ourselves that need fixing.
-Mort Fertel

Satisfaction lies in the effort, not in the attainment. Full effort is full victory.
-Mahatma Gandhi

One is not what he says he is, but what he demonstrates himself to be.
-Unknown

If you are patient in one moment of anger, you will escape a hundred days of sorrow.
-*Chinese Epigram*

Enthusiasm is the vital element toward the individual success of every man or woman.
-Conrad Hilton

The only names people call you that matter are the ones that you answer to.
-Madea, "Madea's Family Reunion"

If you always give, you will always have.
-Chinese proverb

Things turn out best for the people who make the best of the way things turn out.
-John Wooden

Let no feeling of discouragement prey upon you, and in the end you are sure to succeed.
-Abraham Lincoln

Nothing is a waste of time if you use the experience wisely.
-Auguste Rodin

The ultimate measure of a man is not where he stands in moments of comfort and convenience, but where he stands at times of challenge and controversy . . .
-Martin Luther King, Jr.

Whenever you fall, pick something up.
-Oswald Avery

You can tell more about a person by what he says about others than you can by what others say about him.
-Leo Aikman

Often the difference between a successful marriage and a mediocre one consists of leaving about three or four things a day unsaid.
-Harlan Miller

Coincidence is God's way of remaining anonymous.
-Unknown

Joy can only be real if people look upon their life as a service, and have a definite object in life outside themselves and their personal happiness.
-Leonard Tolstoy

Pleasure in the job puts perfection in the work.
-Aristotle

If you want to make peace, you don't talk to your friends. You talk to your enemies.
-*Moshe Dayan*

The value of consistent prayer is not that He will hear us, but that we will hear Him.
-*William McGill*

Sin is like quicksand: Your own efforts only make you sink deeper. Only an outside hand can pull you out.
-*Unknown*

It is better to be a lion for a day than a sheep all your life.
-*Elizabeth Kenny*

The man who removes a mountain begins by carrying away small stones.
-*William Faulkner*

Don't let life discourage you; everyone who got where he is had to begin where he was.
-*Richard L Evans*

When you see God's hands in everything, it is easy to leave everything in God's hands.
-*Unknown*

Worrying is like a rocking chair: it gives you something to do, but it doesn't get you anywhere.
-*Unknown*

We must learn to live together as brothers or perish together as fools.
-*Martin Luther King, Jr.*

Life is ten percent what happens to you and ninety percent how you respond to it.
-*Lou Holtz*

Do not pray for tasks equal to your powers. Pray for power equal to your tasks.
-Phillips Brooks

Nothing lowers the level on conversation more than raising the voice.
-Stanley Horowitz

To admit you were wrong is to declare you are wiser now than before.
-Unknown

Children are likely to live up to what you believe of them.
-Lady Bird Johnson

If I try to be like him, who will be like me?
-Yiddish proverb

We must adjust to changing times and still hold to unchanging principles.
-Jimmy Carter

We ought not to be weary of doing little things for the love of God, who regards not the greatness of the work, but the love with which it is performed.
-Brother Lawrence, The Practice of the Presence of God

Be curious always! For knowledge will not acquire you: you must acquire it.
-Sudie Back

I found out . . . that my personal joy is not somebody else's responsibility. It's my responsibility.
-Joyce Meyer

You cannot push anyone up a ladder unless he is willing to climb himself.
-Andrew Carnegie

Waste no tears over grief of yesterday.
-Euripides

We must make the choices that enable us to fulfill the deepest capacities of our real selves.
-Thomas Merton

Be like a postage stamp. Stick to one thing until you get there.
-Josh Billings

Be who you are and say what you feel, because those who mind don't matter and those who matter don't mind.
-Theodore Geisel

When we are down to nothing, God is up to something.
-Unknown

You miss 100 percent of the shots you never take.
-Wayne Gretzky

From what we get, we can make a living; what we give, however, makes a life.
-Arthur Ashe

Hold fast to dreams, for if dreams die, life is a broken-winged bird that cannot fly.
-Langston Hughes

Efficiency is doing the thing right. Effectiveness is doing the right thing.
-Peter F. Drucker

Depression is nourished by a lifetime of ungrieved and unforgiven hurts.
-Penelope Sweet

Avoiding danger is no safer in the long run than outright exposure.
-Helen Keller

A bit of fragrance always clings to the hand that gives roses.
-Chinese proverb

Courage is resistance to fear, mastery of fear—not absence of fear.
-Mark Twain

Diamonds are nothing more than chunks of coal that stuck to their jobs.
-Malcolm Forbes

Change your thoughts and you change your world.
-Norman Vincent Peale

Try not to become a man of success, but rather try to become a man of value.
-Albert Einstein

It's not whether you get knocked down. It's whether you get back up.
-Vince Lombardi

Do not go where the path may lead, go instead where there is no path and leave a trail.
-Ralph Waldo Emerson

The man who goes farthest is generally the one who is willing to do and dare.
-Dale Carnegie

Love is how you stay alive, even after you are gone.
-Morrie Schwartz

You can do anything—but not everything.
-David Allen

If you are ignorant, the world is going to cheat you; if you are weak, the world is going to kick you; if you are a coward, the world is going to keep you running.
-Benjamin E. May

The importance of one's life is evident in the impact it has on other lives.
-Jackie Robinson

I get up in the morning with one simple goal in mind: to never have a person be worse off than they were before they met me.
-Fred McClure (Tampa partner at law giant DLA Piper)

Our main business is not to see what lies dimly at a distance but to do what lies clearly at hand.
—Thomas Carlyle

Class is an intangible quality that commands rather than demands the respect of others.
-John Wooden

Influences exist at every level, . . . good and bad, but your internal core belief system develops your moral compass and directs you to making life changing decisions. We make decisions and then our decisions make us.
-Chuck Miller

A setback as some might call it is really just an opportunity to find the resolve that we all have but can't seem to get to until the "test" arrives.
-Greg Gaines

More good things are lost by indecision than by the wrong decision.
-Unknown

Faith is a pipeline. It can flow in health, carrying water or oxygen, or it can be filled with poison. What values do you pour through yours?
-Robert Schuller

I cannot imagine how the clockwork of the universe can exist without a Clockmaker.
-Voltaire

Worry not that no one knows of you; seek to be worth knowing.
-Confucius

$\mathscr{H}$bout the Author:

Conditioning for excellence has been the theme of Tim's life since childhood. Reaching beyond the norm and preparing to dwell amongst the best in whatever objectives he chose has guided his path to success. As a three-sport (football, basketball, and track) athlete and honors student at Peach County High School in Fort Valley, GA, Tim excelled on the field of play and in the classroom. Upon graduating in 1988, he received a number of college scholarship offers for football. He chose Howard University over more auspicious football programs. At Howard, Tim continued a successful scholastic and football career. He has the distinction of being the first Athlete in the history of Howard University to be named to the GTE Academic All-America Team. Tim was also named All-Conference, All-American, and Defensive Player of the Year in each of his final two college seasons. His scholastic honors include being chosen by the Graduate School of Arts and Sciences to participate in the National Name Exchange for outstanding academic achievement by juniors and seniors, and selection as a lifetime member of the Golden Key International Honour Society. Tim completed a Bachelor's Degree in Fashion Merchandising and Business Marketing 1992, followed by post-graduate studies in Athletic Administration. In 2005, Tim was honored with induction into the Howard Athletics Hall of Fame.

The Green Bay Packers selected Tim in the 1993 NFL Draft. He went on to have a well-traveled 7-year professional football career, playing alongside such NFL legends as Joe Montana, Marcus Allen, and Ronnie Lott. During his career he served as a Captain for both the Kansas City Chiefs and Philadelphia Eagles.

In reaching the pinnacle of his career Tim met the anticipated obstacles and detractors. However, he believed that nothing could stand in the way of his achieving greatness. He credits proper preparation, attitude, motivation, relationships, and information for his continued success.

Tim has been able to catapult his personal business ventures by applying the wisdom from the "gridiron" and everyday life. In addition to life coaching and speaking engagements, Tim serves as a Financial Services Specialist with State Farm Insurance. In this role, he helps Agents in their Good Neighbor pledge by teaching financial services strategies for the underserved markets of middle America. With an enduring passion for helping others, he shares his business insights, life-skills, and sales expertise from an entertaining, engaging, and unique perspective. With a passionate and frank delivery style, Tim has become an invaluable resource for companies, sports teams, schools, and youth organizations. Answering the call to the ministry of Jesus Christ, Tim was ordained Non-denominationally in the spring of 2002. He is also a Certified Life Coach, Small Business Coach, Corporate Wellness Coach, Certified Personal Fitness Trainer, and Certified Training Director.

Tim and wife Audrey live in Atlanta, GA. He's also the proud father of three children: Tre' (7/96), Lexi (7/97), and Christian (5/99). The Watsons remain active in their local community through charitable work via involvement with the NFL Alumni Association, The Tampa Beautification Program (on whose Board of Trustees Tim serves), their local church, and their personal philanthropic organization (UPLIFT Excellence Foundation, Inc.) which annually provides food and toys to families in need during the Thanksgiving and Christmas holidays.

Tim gives back to local youth by coaching and sponsoring youth football and track programs, instructing youth sports camps, and conducting life-skills seminars for young students and scholar-athletes. He is also honored to be a made man of Omega Psi Phi Fraternity, Inc. In addition to being a leader in the business, Tim has served in several volunteer leadership positions; including serving as Co-Chair (with wife, Audrey) of UPLIFT Excellence Foundation, Inc. (1994—Present), League Director for the Air Raid Football Organization of Arizona NYS (2001-2005), President of the Talas Homeowners Association, an exclusive upscale community in Peoria, AZ (2001-2003), and President of the NFL Alumni Tampa Chapter (2007—2009).

TIM'S PROFESSIONAL CAREER AT A GLANCE:

- 1993-1999: Professional Football Player-Safety, Green Bay Packers, Kansas City Chiefs, New York Giants, Barcelona Dragons (NFLE), Philadelphia Eagles, Arizona Rattlers (AFL).
- 1999-2001: Financial Services Professional, MONY Sports Financial Services.
- 1998-2006: President/Business Manager/Training Director, UPLIFT Properties Group, LLC.
- 2006-Present: Agency Field Recruiter-Atlanta Metro Area (8/2011—Present); Financial Services Specialist-Florida Zone, State Farm Insurance.
- 2003-Present: Life Coach, Professional Motivational Speaker Business Consultant, & Published Author—UPLIFT Systems, LLC.